INTRODUCTION

Down through the years, I've always been very careful when writing songs for a recording. I want to say clearly and specifically what the Lord has put on my heart to say. Many times, that particular message has to do with what message the Lord wants to get across to the body of believers I will be standing before that year.

In this particular season of my life and ministry, I sense the Holy Spirit saying that the time of the end is coming much sooner than we think. He wants us to focus on winning souls more than ever before. Therefore, many songs on my *Mission 3:16* album have to deal with the conversion experience.

Now I've written this *Mission 3:16 Devotional* to fan the evangelistic fire God has placed in our hearts. Our first priority as believers is to go out and do the great commission Jesus gave to us in Matthew 28:18-20:

> **And Jesus came and spake unto them, saying, All power is given unto me in heaven and in earth. Go ye therefore, and teach all nations, baptizing them in the name of the Father, and of the Son, and of the Holy Ghost: Teaching them to observe all things whatsoever I have commanded you: and, lo, I am with**

you alway, even unto the end of the world.
Amen.

A commission is "an authorization to perform certain duties or tasks...authority to act on behalf of another...a group of people officially appointed to perform specified duties."[1] And the number one scripture I know about sharing the message of salvation is John 3:16:

> *For God so loved the world, that he gave his only begotten Son, that whosoever believeth in him should not perish, but have everlasting life.*

That is our mission: to share the most famous, well known, and important 3:16 ever known to man. Whether you are in school, at work, or having fun at the beach, tell people what Jesus has done for you. Invite them to church or a concert — one of mine if possible! Pray for them when they're down or not feeling well. And when the Spirit leads you, ask them if they want to accept Jesus as their Lord and Savior.

It's my prayer that this devotional will help YOU to stay focused and stirred up about YOUR vital part in OUR MISSION 3:16.

---

[1] *Webster's New World Collegiate Dictionary* (New York: Macmillian, 1988), p. 280.

Mission 3:16 Devotional

by

Carman

ALBURY PUBLISHING
Tulsa, Oklahoma

Mission 3:16 Devotional
ISBN 1-57778-098-1
Copyright © 1998 by Carman Ministries
P. O. Box 5093
Brentwood, Tennessee 37024-5093

Published by ALBURY PUBLISHING
P. O. Box 470406
Tulsa, Oklahoma 74147-0406

MISSION 3:16

WE CAN'T CONTAIN WHAT'S INSIDE
THUNDER AND LIGHTNING CAN'T HIDE
FREED FROM THE PAST
DESTINED TO WIN
TAKING THE GOSPEL WHERE IT'S NEVER BEEN

Chorus

WE'RE ON, WE'RE ON, WE'RE ON A MISSION
AND WE'LL GO
WHERE THE BRAVE
DARE TO FLY
WE'RE ON A MISSION
AND WE KNOW IT'S A RACE DO OR DIE
TO KNOW HIM AND MAKE HIM KNOWN IS OUR CREED
LETTING THE FIRE BE FREED
MISSION 3:16

WE DONT KNOW WHAT WE WILL FIND
DEEP BEHIND ENEMY LINES
WE ARE THE CALLED WE ARE THE FEW
READY TO SERVE HIM AND WILLING TO DO

Repeat Chorus

HE DID NOT COME INTO THE WORLD
BUT TO SAVE US
HE CAME SO HE COULD SET US FREE
NOT ENSLAVE US

FREELY WE RECEIVED
FREELY WE MUST GIVE
THE MESSAGE OF SALVATION TO LIVE
YES TO LIVE

Repeat Chorus

MISSION POSSIBLE

EIGHTEEN HUNDRED YEARS HAVE ROLLED AWAY SINCE THE SON OF GOD, OUR BLESSED REDEEMER, OFFERED HIMSELF ON MOUNT CALVARY FOR THE SALVATION OF OUR SPECIES; AND MORE THAN HALF OF MANKIND STILL CONTINUE TO DENY HIS DIVINE MISSION AND THE TRUTH OF HIS SACRED WORD.

— HENRY CLAY, 1829

Your mission, should you choose to accept it, is not a Mission Impossible, but a Mission Possible, Mission Probable, and Mission Perfect — designed uniquely for you. No matter what your limitations, if you choose to accept this mission, you will be able to fulfill it.

A mission is a specific task a person is assigned to do. When God placed you in space as part of the human race, you came "on assignment" from heaven. Remember you are here on purpose, for a purpose, in divine purpose. Before the foundation of the earth, about the same time God the Father was deciding to send His Son Jesus, He decided to send you. In the fullness of time He then formed you in your mother's womb to be equipped with everything you would need for your mission.

You may not have decided what career you want. You may not have chosen a mate. Maybe you feel as if your life has no direction at all and you are just going wherever "fate" dictates. Well, until you get more specific instructions from the Holy Spirit, He has already told you in the Word of God about your most important mission — winning souls and discipling believers.

Have you been ignoring your assignment from God's Word? If so, you have been missing an adventure! The Great Commission is the adventure of your life!

You can boldly charge into enemy territory and snatch kidnapped royalty from hell's flames. You can dangle from a wire and reach into the pits of hell to grasp the hand of one lost soul. You can be tethered from a plane, holding a life jacket for one backslider trapped in the swirling waters of sin.

It is an adventure. It is YOUR mission. Choose to accept it today!

PURPOSE

> YOU POSSESS THE CAPACITY TO BE
> A LEADER WITHIN THE SPHERE OF THE
> PURPOSE FOR WHICH YOU WERE BORN.
> YOUR PLANS MAY CHANGE,
> BUT YOUR PURPOSE IS CONSTANT.
>
> — MYLES MUNROE

You were born pregnant with potential and programmed for a unique purpose. God did not simply drop you from heaven. You did not just fall through time and space into this place where you now live. Your existence was designed by God long before you landed. You see, God always has a plan. Even when mankind fails, as Adam and Eve did in the Garden of Eden, God has a back-up plan.

John recorded in Revelation 13:8 that the Lamb (Jesus) was "slain from the foundation of the world." Before Adam named the animals, before Eve walked her beautiful self up to that tree and had that course-changing conversation with the ultimate creepy-crawler, God had a plan — redemption for man.

Everything God does or has ever done has a purpose. God does nothing outside of purpose. God moves only in regard to purpose. The course of time and space and everything since then that relates to our universe God did ON purpose, IN purpose, FOR purpose, ABOUT purpose, or BECAUSE OF purpose.

Have you ever asked yourself, "Why am I here? What is my reason for being? What is my purpose?" Many people ask themselves these questions every day. Some feel they have meaningless lives, but the Bible tells them a different story.

> *My frame was not hidden from you when I was made in the secret place. When I was woven together in the depths of the earth, your eyes saw my unformed body. All the days ordained for me were written in your book before one of them came to be.*
>
> **Psalm 139:15-16** NIV

God has had a plan and a purpose for you since before you were even conceived. If you haven't asked Him what that is, right now is the time. And once He tells you, ask Him what's the first step — and then take it!

STIR UP THE GIFT

IF THERE BE A DESTINY, IT IS OF NO
AVAIL FOR US UNLESS WE WORK WITH IT.
— CALVIN COOLIDGE

Before I made Jesus the Lord of my life, I used to sing and play the guitar in nightclubs. Well, maybe nightclub isn't the right word — they were bars. Bar is really the best word, since most of the people there were in captivity! One evening I heard a man order a martini. He wanted it "shaken, not stirred."

My curiosity got the best of me, and later I asked the bartender if there was a difference between shaken and stirred or was this guy just showing off. The bartender told me that a drink was shaken instead of stirred to keep from bruising the alcohol. I laughed at the thought that alcohol could be "bruised," considering all the damage I had seen alcohol do. I could not imagine it ever being fragile. Years later I would begin to see the spiritual parallel to this concept as it related to Christians.

Often we sit in church and hear a missionary speak. We watch their slides of lost humanity in the darkened corners of the globe and we are shaken. We

feel the needs and so we give in the offering and quietly thank God that He did not call us to that foreign
field.

We are shaken, but not stirred.

> **Wherefore I put thee in remembrance that
> thou stir up the gift of God, which is in thee by
> the putting on of my hands.**
>
> **2 Timothy 1:6**

Stir yourself up this week, fan the embers of your
smoldering faith. I think you know how to do that, but
just in case you've forgotten: get rid of sin and anything that keeps you from God. Stay in church, read
the Word, pray without ceasing — you know the drill!
When you are fully ablaze you will find all the power,
love, and self-discipline you need to fulfill your
Mission 3:16.

FEAR NOT

> THE ONLY THING WE HAVE TO FEAR
> IS FEAR ITSELF.
> — FRANKLIN DELANO ROOSEVELT

"**F**ear and fear alone" is an injury sufficient to cause death, according to a federal court jury in Seattle. Ralph Thompson, third mate on the steamship *Chena*, died of shock the day after his vessel was driven into the center of Valdez, Alaska, by a tidal wave. An insurance company refused to pay accidental death benefits because Thompson had suffered no apparent injuries. However, the court concluded that Thompson had died of fright and it held the company liable.

Has fear kept you from fulfilling your Mission 3:16? Are you "scared to death" to tell someone about Jesus? If you are full of fear, it has not come from God! The enemy of your soul wants to keep you in bondage to fear, thus keeping you out of his territory. He knows that fear can be fatal to your mission, so that's why he spends most of his time trying to intimidate and worry you.

The good news is, God knows this! And He has

charged His Word with powerful promises to overcome all fear and anxiety. The fear of man is a snare (see Proverbs 29:25) and you do not need to fear anything that man might do to you (see Hebrews 13:6). These promises are God's Word to YOU.

> *For you did not receive a spirit that makes you a slave again to fear, but you received the Spirit of sonship.*
>
> *Romans 8:15 NIV*

You may be challenged by the awesome mission before you, but NEVER FEAR. God is near and He will keep you on track as you focus your faith on Him, take courage, and appropriate His strength for your task.

Try this exercise this week. Each day find five "fear not"s in your Bible. I found eighty of them just today. Write them down and drive all fear out of your life by reminding yourself of the power, love, and sound mind God has promised!

FORGET ABOUT IT!

NO WORRIES FOR THE REST OF OUR DAYS — HAKUNA MATATA!

— FROM THE FILM, *LION KING*

When the downhearted lion cub Simba was giving up on his future because of his past, the wart hog Pumbaa gave him some misquoted but accurate advice, "My buddy Timon says, 'You gotta put your behind in your past.'"

What Timon actually said was, "You gotta put your past behind you." Either way you say it, it all boils down to "Forget about it!"

Forgetting what is behind and straining toward what is ahead, I press on toward the goal to win the prize for which God has called me heavenward in Christ Jesus.
Philippians 3:13-14 NIV

My pastor used to talk about the buzzard. Buzzards are experts at digging up anything that is dead. Buzzards sniff out death, dig it up, and chew on it. UGH!

Now Satan is the ultimate buzzard. He wants to dig up everything he can find on you that could bring death into your life. He and his cohorts are out to get you and they are more threatening than any tabloid magazine ever could be. Satan will constantly remind you of your past in order to retard your future.

Satan knows that if he can keep you living in your behind — I mean, in your past — he can stop you from completing your mission. After all, how can you reach others with the message of forgiveness if you cannot forgive yourself? Remember, that's the whole point of your Mission 3:16: YOU ARE FORGIVEN!

Therefore if any man be in Christ, he is a new creature: old things are passed away; behold, all things are become new.

2 Corinthians 5:17

Forget those things which are behind. Forget about it! And in the immortal words of Timon and Pumbaa, "Hakuna Matata!" Only by total surrender of your past to God will you truly be able to have "No Worries!"

PEOPLE OF GOD

I was inspired to write this song after participation in the "March for Jesus" through the streets of Nashville. It just sounds like a group of people on a quest, with a marching band, waving banners, and standing up for righteousness.

WE'RE THE PEOPLE OF GOD, AND WE'RE HERE TO SAY
LIVING FOR THE LORD IS THE BETTER WAY
WE'RE THE PEOPLE OF GOD, AND WE'RE ON A QUEST
RAISING UP A BANNER OF RIGHTEOUSNESS

FULL OF HOPE, FAITH, AND FIRE
WE'RE THE CHOSEN, RISING TO A HIGHER PLANE
A PERFORMANCE, STIRRING UP THE GIFT THAT
    WAS DORMANT
WAR, NO, WE'RE NOT AFRAID
SEND A GIANT OUT, WE'LL TAKE HIM DOWN WITH
    THE WORD, AND SPIRIT
THIS GENERATION NEEDS TO HEAR IT NOW
AND DEMONSTRATED WITH GOD'S POWER

EXTRA, EXTRA READ ALL ABOUT IT
SATAN LOST THE WAR AND NO DOUBT IT WORKS

THIS HOLY POWER AND IT'S OURS TO DEVOUR FOES
WHO COME AGAINST US 'CAUSE IT SENDS US OUT
AND STRONG IN THE SPIRIT
THIS GENERATION NEEDS TO HEAR IT NOW
AND DEMONSTRATED WITH GOD'S POWER

SOMEONE HURTS US, HE'S THE ONE WHO MENDS US
GOD BEFORE US, WHO CAN BE AGAINST US
REDEMPTION, YES, WE'RE LIVING PROOF
WE'RE THE CHURCH, CHURCH ON THE MOVE

YOU ARE FULL OF IT!

I HEARD A FINE EXAMPLE TODAY, NAMELY, THAT HIS EXCELLENCY GENERAL WASHINGTON RODE AROUND AMONG HIS ARMY YESTERDAY AND ADMONISHED EACH AND EVERY ONE TO FEAR GOD, TO PUT AWAY THE WICKEDNESS THAT HAS SET IN AND BECOME SO GENERAL, AND TO PRACTICE THE CHRISTIAN VIRTUES.

— HENRY MUHLENBERG,
LUTHERAN PASTOR AT VALLEY FORGE

When someone tells you that you are "full of it," that is probably not meant as a compliment! But I think it is time for Christians to be full of it — the Holy Ghost, that is! If we are really people of God, we should be so full of Him that He spills out all over everyone we meet.

If a full cup of liquid is moved even a little, whatever it contains spills out. In the same way, when life's circumstances jar us even a tiny bit, our true nature spills out. If we are full of *ourselves*, out comes, "I can't help it. I'm Italian and we have always had quick tempers." Well, the truth of the matter is, we are simply full of the flesh!

But we know from the Word that God is loving, patient, kind, and forgiving. He is full of wisdom and power. He is also holy and just. If we are truly people of God and we are full of Him, we will overflow with *His* nature and character.

> **A good man out of the good treasure of his heart bringeth forth that which is good; and an evil man out of the evil treasure of his heart bringeth forth that which is evil: for of the abundance of the heart his mouth speaketh.**
>
> **Luke 6:45**

What have you been overflowing with and spilling out lately?

If your spiritual checkup proves you to be a quart low on the Spirit of God, then pull yourself up to the Holy Ghost filling station and get a fresh tank full. You will soon find that the stuff you were full of has been replaced with the character and nature of God. Then when you start spilling over onto people, they'll experience Jesus!

FAITH

FAITH GIVES US COURAGE TO FACE THE
UNCERTAINTIES OF THE FUTURE.
— MARTIN LUTHER KING, JR.

People of God are to be full of faith. Romans 12:3 tells us that we have each been given a measure of it. In the simplest of terms, faith is abandoning ourselves to God.

F For
A All
I I
T Trust
H Him

We do so many things in faith, but we do not often recognize that we are operating in faith. Each time you turn on a light switch or a faucet you expect, in faith, that you will have power or water. After all, you have tried it before and it has always worked.

But when it comes to the things of God, we are so unsure, and we often fail to exercise the measure of faith we have been given. We look around at others and feel like God used a measuring cup for their faith, but for us He used a teaspoon — or worse yet, an eye dropper! Jesus said in Matthew 17:20 that all we needed was faith the size of a grain of mustard seed (which is an extremely small seed) to speak to a mountain and it would move.

True people of God don't settle for mustard seed faith.

They increase their faith by hearing and reading the Word of God. (See Romans 10:17.) True people of God make every effort to add to their faith. (See 2 Peter 1:5.) True people of God operate in faith birthed from the love of God that has been shed abroad in their hearts. (See Romans 5:5.)

You've got it and the world needs it.

Stir yourself up in your most holy faith this week and take it to the streets — to the people around you who need Jesus. You have the faith you need, so add to it and then get out there and make a difference in your world!

HOPE

WE DID NOT DARE TO
BREATHE A PRAYER
OR GIVE OUR ANGUISH SCOPE!
SOMETHING WAS DEAD IN
EACH OF US,
AND WHAT WAS DEAD WAS HOPE.
— OSCAR WILDE

Oscar Wilde was widely known for his flamboyant style. A drama he wrote, based on the life of Salome (the dancing girl who was responsible for the beheading of John the Baptist) was considered scandalous. He also wrote fairy tales, comedies, and anarchic political essays. But with all of his gifts and talents, he lacked hope.

Wilde was well-educated and sought-after in social circles, including the royal family of England, because of his creative genius, flair, and brilliant mind. However, he was also a homosexual. The father of Wilde's homosexual lover sent him into social and financial ruin with a lawsuit that ended in imprisonment. Oscar Wilde was sentenced to two years in prison for his homosexual offenses, then later died in exile. What a tragedy! Even the most gifted life can have no hope.

Today the world says there is no hope. Society is darker than ever. More and more countries are testing their nuclear power. We now have terrorists right here in America. Highway and hallway shootings are reported daily. Even with the greatest medical advances, disease is rampant. Natural disasters are increasing, and the diminishing rain forests are threatening the very air we breathe. It is no wonder the world feels hopeless.

> *Seeing then that we have such hope, we use great plainness of speech.*
>
> **2 Corinthians 3:12**

HOWEVER, as a child of the King you should be full of the *blessed hope.* Share Jesus with someone today, and give them hope! The Word commands us to get out there and tell the world plainly and simply that no matter what they are going through, Jesus has the answer. He is their answer! And when people have the answer, they have hope.

FIRE

> ### LIFE IS NOT TRIED; IT'S MERELY SURVIVED IF YOU ARE STANDING OUTSIDE THE FIRE.
> — GARTH BROOKS

Fires in the natural realm can be devastating. They are all-consuming and have no respect for life or property. If you are in their path, you will be burned.

Many firefighters fight fire with fire. They set a backfire which will burn toward the first fire. When the fires meet, they will consume each other. Recently Florida firefighters used the same strategy to try to stop the state from being completely destroyed by numerous massive fires.

When we look at the condition of the world today, it is not difficult to realize that it is ablaze with sin. Every evil work spoken of in Scripture seems to be burning and out of control right before our eyes. And it seems that the more strategies and plans we have to put the fire out, the more it burns out of control. The Moral Majority has not put it out. Legislation can't stop it. All the best efforts of men to douse the raging fires of sin have had little impact.

It is time for Holy Ghost, fire-filled believers to set a backfire!

Our God is an all-consuming fire, and His power dwells in YOU.

For too long we have been quenching the fire of the Holy Spirit and merely surviving, while Satan's flames lap up everything around us. But the Church is beginning to wake up and realize that it will take the fire of the Holy Ghost to cause Satan's plans to back-fire on him.

John answered them all, "I baptize you with water. But one more powerful than I will come, the thongs of whose sandals I am not worthy to untie. He will baptize you with the Holy Spirit and with fire."

Luke 3:16 NIV

Get fired up! Stir up the flame that is within your spirit. Together we can set the world ablaze for Jesus Christ and drive the devil out!

THE STANDARD

> "BANNER: A PIECE OF CLOTH BEARING A DESIGN, MOTTO, SLOGAN, ETC., SOMETIMES ATTACHED TO A STAFF AND USED AS A BATTLE STANDARD."
> — WEBSTER'S NEW WORLD COLLEGE DICTIONARY

From Afghanistan to Zimbabwe, every nation and principality, many organizations, and some families have a banner that is the official standard of their people. The Danish flag, consisting of a large white cross on a red field, is the oldest national flag in existence. According to a legend, a red banner bearing a white cross appeared in the sky at a most critical moment during a crusade against pagans, led by Valdemar II of Denmark. The flag created from that legend has been the national emblem of Denmark since the thirteenth century.

Long before the Danes ever saw their banner in the sky, God established the first banner over His people. In Exodus 17:15 we find our personal banner, *Jehovah Nissi* — the Lord our banner, our victory. As people of God we are covered by *Jehovah Nissi*. As long as we operate under His banner we are assured victory. When we move out from under His covering, that's when we get into big trouble.

> ***Thou hast given a banner to them that fear thee, that it may be displayed because of the truth.***
>
> ***Psalm 60:4***

God's standard has been set, and I want to hold it high. I want to represent the victorious people of God in every word and deed. As long as I name the name of Jesus, I represent God's glorious kingdom. If I don't hold up the standard, the banner of righteousness, I cannot be part of the people of God.

What flag flies over the kingdom of your heart? Maybe it is time to check your flag pole to see what banner you have been waving for the world to see. As people of God, we represent the Messiah and the promises of victory, peace, and prosperity that He brings to the world. All you have to do is wave the flag, and people will be on your doorstep asking for help — His name is Jesus!

LEGENDARY MISSION

Tony Orlando and I became like father and son during my concert series in Branson, Missouri. I would sing the Gospel and he'd evangelize the other entertainers on the strip by bringing them to the concert. What a team! It's only appropriate that he'd sing the theme of the album:

FOR GOD SO LOVED THE WORLD,

THAT HE GAVE HIS ONLY BEGOTTEN SON,

THAT WHOSOEVER BELIEVETH IN HIM

SHOULD NOT PERISH,

BUT HAVE EVERLASTING LIFE.

COLUMBUS

> MY HOPE IN THE ONE WHO CREATED ALL SUSTAINS ME; HE IS AN EVER PRESENT HELP IN TROUBLE... WHEN I AM EXTREMELY DEPRESSED, HE RAISED ME WITH HIS RIGHT HAND, SAYING, "O MAN OF LITTLE FAITH, GET UP, IT IS I; DO NOT BE AFRAID."
>
> — CHRISTOPHER COLUMBUS

I have always been impressed with Christopher Columbus' life and legendary mission. When I was a child I was so excited to find out that this great man of faith and adventure was an Italian like me. I believed that all he accomplished was because he was from a race of determined and focused people.

Today, as I look over the history of his life, I see that he *was* from a race of determined and focused people — the people of God. And God had an incredible mission for him — to find a home for believers who would be persecuted for their faith, a place where they could worship God freely.

Though some history books have omitted information about Columbus' deep religious faith, others have noted that he includes God in practically all of his writings. After reading what he wrote, you get a strong sense that he wrote from his own personal dependence and trust in the Creator of the universe.

> ***My meat is to do the will of him that sent me, and to finish his work.***
> ***John 4:34***

Like Columbus, I want my life's mission to stand for Christ. I want to be a reflection in word and deed of the One who assigned my mission.

Is everything you do reflecting your faith in and walk with God?

Even if you are not yet fully aware of the scope of your mission, are you walking daily as an adventurer in faith? You may be destined for the history books! You never know all God has prepared for you to accomplish.

JOHN GLENN

THE VIEW WAS TREMENDOUS. I COULD
SEE FOR HUNDREDS OF MILES IN EVERY
DIRECTION — THE SUN ON WHITE
CLOUDS, PATCHES OF BLUE WATER
BENEATH AND GREAT CHUNKS OF
FLORIDA AND THE SOUTHEASTERN U.S.

— JOHN GLENN

John Glenn's legendary mission happened February 20, 1962, when he boarded the Mercury spacecraft *Friendship 7*. This mission lasted only 4 hours, 55 minutes, as he orbited the earth three times. We cannot begin to comprehend the training and discipline he had to go through to prepare for this seemingly short mission — one that would impact all future space travel.

Glenn's experience not only changed the world, it changed him. It gave him a new view of the world, a broader perspective on his life and his priorities. You see, his mission was not perfect. His life was threatened when his heat shield for re-entry came loose. His mission proved so heroic that after he landed safely back on earth he was honored with a ticker tape parade, much like the one thrown for Charles Lindbergh after he had flown the Atlantic in 1927.

God has a great number of assignments for your life. You will have many missions. You will learn some of them from His Word, such as reaching the lost, and some of them from the Holy Spirit, such as reaching out to a particular person. Some will last your lifetime and others for short periods of time. Many will not seem legendary to mankind, but every assignment completed for the kingdom of God will be legendary to YOU and to HIM.

If you are serving God with your whole heart and obeying His directives daily, you are, right now, fulfilling your legendary mission. Perhaps, like John Glenn, you need to go on a journey above the circumstances of your life just now. Get God's perspective on your place in His scheme of things. Look over the vast expanse of the universe and begin to imagine all the great and glorious things God has planned for you.

MOTHER TERESA

I NEVER DOUBTED THAT I'VE DONE THE
RIGHT THING. IT WAS THE WILL OF GOD.
IT WAS HIS CHOICE.

— MOTHER TERESA

Born in 1910 in Macedonia, Agnes Gonxha Bojaxhiu (Mother Teresa) grew up under the threat of war as the Albanians rose up against the Turks. Despite difficult times, her mother, who was a dressmaker, found time to help the poor. As a young girl, Agnes began to go with her mother to visit the sick, the shut-in, and the lonely. These early days as a caregiver brought out a tenderness for those less fortunate in Agnes. By the age of eighteen, she had a passionate determination to dedicate her life to serving God.

After a six-week stay in Ireland to study English, Agnes arrived in Calcutta in January 1929. In 1931 she took her vows in the Catholic Church, taking the name Sister Teresa. She chose the name after Therese, the patron saint of missionaries. Though St. Therese had lived only to the age of tewenty-four, Mother Teresa would carry on her mission for decades.

Though Mother Teresa began her service to God as a teacher, her mission eventually took her to the poverty-ridden streets of Calcutta, giving food, clothing, and dignity to society's discards, "the poorest of the poor." In outlining the duties for her newly formed order, she set simple guidelines: Go to the poorest of the poor, visit them continuously, show them Jesus Christ's love for them and awaken their response to His great love by feeding, clothing, and loving them.

She lived in the belief that the moment we give something to God in prayer it becomes infinite. Today her work continues. Though she has gone on to her eternal reward, her mission continues because she gave herself and her ministry to God.

Remember: the same is true of your mission. Every life you touch for Jesus Christ becomes an eternal reward.

MARTIN LUTHER KING JR.

> I PERCEIVED IMMEDIATELY THAT THIS
> BOY — FIFTEEN YEARS OLD — WAS
> MATURE BEYOND HIS YEARS, THAT HE
> SPOKE AS A MAN WHO SHOULD HAVE
> HAD TEN MORE YEARS EXPERIENCE THAN
> WAS POSSIBLE. HE HAD A BALANCE AND
> GRASP OF LIFE AND ITS PROBLEMS THAT
> EXCEEDED THAT.
>
> — BENJAMIN MAYS,
> EULOGIZING DR. MARTIN LUTHER KING JR.

As a young man, Martin Luther King Jr. recognized the urgency of making a difference for his people as well as for oppressed people of every race. His mission would not be an easy one, and it would eventually take his life. However, his legendary mission is still affecting lives today.

It is never too early to get a vision for your mission.

David communicated with God while he tended sheep as a young boy, and killed a lion and a bear in the power of God. Young Joseph received dreams from God that he would one day be a great ruler over Israel.

As a very small boy Samuel heard God calling his name while he served in the temple.

> **MY CHALLENGE TO THE YOUNG PEOPLE IS TO PICK UP WHERE THIS GENERATION HAS LEFT OFF TO CREATE A WORLD WHERE EVERY MAN, WOMAN, AND CHILD IS NOT LIMITED, EXCEPT BY THEIR OWN CAPABILITIES.**
>
> — COLIN POWELL

You too can hear from God regarding your life's mission, even if you are very young. The prophet Isaiah recorded that your eye has not seen nor has your ear heard all God has prepared for you if you will "wait on" or pray and listen to Him. (See Isaiah 64:4.) He did not say, "Unless you are too young."

If you want to know your mission, begin to wait on the Lord. You are not too young, too unprepared, too scarred by life's circumstances, too dumb, or too poor to fulfill His mission for your life. Whatever you are lacking, God will provide it, because it's His mission for you!

Wait on God this week. Read His Word and listen for His voice. Then rise up and obey what He has said!

JESUS CHRIST

> MAN, WHO NEEDED A PURPOSE, A
> MISSION, TO KEEP HIM ALIVE, HAD ONE.
> HE COULD BE...GOD'S CO-WORKER....
> — GEORGE WASHINGTON CARVER

The most legendary of all missions, of course, was Jesus'. He came to earth in the form of a baby, grew up experiencing the same heartaches and pressures all human beings face, but He did not sin. And Scripture tells us that Jesus experienced every temptation any human being has ever faced. (See Hebrews 4:15.) He had to feed a hungry staff, pay taxes, settle disagreements among His disciples, endure the death of His cousin, John the Baptist, and was betrayed by one of His disciples. He put heart and soul into His ministry, and yet even many of His own family did not recognize Him as the Messiah.

Jesus is our supreme example of mission behavior. He knew when to speak and when to be silent. He knew when to challenge and when to forgive. He knew when to rebuke and the right reasons for doing so. He knew how to control His anger and how to be free from roots of bitterness that could have entangled Him. He knew how to recognize evil and defeat Satan's attacks. Jesus faced what you are facing *right now* and He had a victorious mission. You can too!

"How?" you ask. "I mean, He was God and I'm not."

Jesus walked and talked with His Father God, and you walk and talk with your Father God. And the power of the Holy Spirit anointed Him the same way He anoints us today:

> ***The Spirit of the Lord is upon me, because he hath anointed me to preach the gospel to the poor.***
>
> ***Luke 4:18***

Romans 8:11 says that the same Spirit who resurrected Jesus from the dead dwells in YOU! And Jesus told us in John 14:12 that we would do even greater works than He did, that the Father would send the Holy Spirit to be with us and help us (see John 14:16).

So you see, the same Holy Spirit who helped Jesus is *in* you and *upon* you to help you succeed in your mission. You can do it!

NEVER BE

Sometimes when you're at your worst and you feel totally forgotten, the Lord shows up the strongest. This song is from the heart because I have lived it myself.

> NEVER BE A HEART THAT HE
> COULDN'T MEND EACH BROKEN PIECE
> NEVER BE A WOUNDED SOUL HE WOULD IGNORE
> THERE'LL NEVER BE A TIME THAT HE
> WOULD EVER TURN HIS BACK ON ME
> THERE'LL NEVER BE A LIFE HE CAN'T RESTORE
>
> WHERE DO YOU GO WHEN YOU FEEL LIKE
> YOU'VE BEEN FORSAKEN
> PURELY FORGOTTEN, ALL ALONE?
> WHAT DO YOU DO WHEN YOUR DREAMS HAVE
> BEEN BROKEN AND SHATTERED
> DOES IT REALLY MATTER TO ANYONE?
> THERE IS A MAN STANDING WITH ARMS OPEN WIDE
> DRYING THE TEARS THAT I'VE CRIED
> LOVING ME AND GIVING LIFE
> AND THERE'LL …
>
> NEVER WILL I DOUBT AGAIN
> I WILL NEVER BE WITHOUT A FRIEND
> NEVER WILL MY EYES FAIL TO SEE
> WHAT THE LORD DID FOR ME
> AND THERE'LL …

DEFEATING LONELINESS

LONELINESS IS THE ULTIMATE POVERTY.
— ABIGAIL VAN BUREN

So many people are struggling today with the feelings of loneliness. Many feel abandoned, forgotten, and unloved. In our humanness, sometimes we will feel lonely, but we are never alone. In Hebrews 13:5, Paul reminds us that Jesus promised to never leave us or forsake us. Then in verse 6, we see that God is our helper and friend, that we do not need to be afraid of anything man can do to us. David said in Psalm 27:10 that even if his mother and father left him, the Lord would adopt him.

Believe me, in my ministry and calling, I have had to learn how to deal with loneliness. It's especially hard when I have to make very difficult decisions; decisions that will not only affect those who work in the ministry and expect a regular paycheck to support their families, but also those who may not be saved if I make the wrong move.

In the midst of the R.I.O.T. tour, I was never more discouraged. In fact, I was sick for weeks over the situation. The tour was not paying for itself, and if we completed it, by the end we would be one million dollars in the hole — but we'd also be able to win ten thousand souls into the kingdom.

My answer came when the Lord asked me the simple question, "Are ten thousand souls worth one million dollars?" But then I heard a more personal question: "Are ten thousand souls worth *your* million dollars? Would you, Carman, be willing to sell everything your ministry has accumulated down through the years to win another ten thousand souls?" In the midst of that fire my answer to the Lord was, "Yes! Absolutely yes!" And suddenly my path was clear again and my peace restored.

If you are feeling forsaken, forgotten, and alone today, cry out to God. He is right there, waiting to hear and to answer — just like He was for me during the R.I.O.T. tour. And you will learn what I have learned through the years: Jesus is always there for you.

> *For he [Jesus] hath said, I will never leave thee, nor forsake thee.*
>
> *Hebrews 13:5*

NEVER TOO LATE

> MY PRINCIPLES HAVE POISONED
> MY FRIEND; MY EXTRAVAGANCE HAS
> BEGGARED MY BOY; MY UNKINDNESS
> HAS MURDERED MY WIFE. AND IS THERE
> ANOTHER HELL? OH, THOU
> BLASPHEMED, YET MOST INDULGENT
> LORD GOD! HELL IS A REFUGE IF IT
> HIDES ME FROM THY FROWN.
> — ALTAMONT, AN ATHEIST ON HIS DEATHBED

This guy was obviously in very bad shape! Unfortunately, he believed a lie that most unbelievers who go to hell believe — that they have sunk too low for God to forgive them. I wish I had been with this man when he died, because I would have told him that there is no sin too great for God to forgive.

As you venture out to accomplish your Mission 3:16, you are going to meet some people who are like Altamont, and they may not be on their deathbed. They may still be causing lots of trouble and making life miserable for themselves and everyone around them. Some people are so deceived by the enemy, they believe they might as well act like the devil because there is no way they can change. They are trapped in their culture, their environment, and their way of thinking and doing things.

That is where you come in! You are the light to shine in their darkness. When you enter their world in the power of God, speaking His truth into their situation, and taking authority over the enemy so he cannot lie to them anymore, the light will expose the lies and the deception will be shattered. You are the guide sent from heaven to show them the way out of their hopeless, helpless life and into a living, loving, dynamic relationship with a Father God who loves them.

The next time you meet someone who is living like the devil, who believes there is no hope for them, DO NOT GIVE UP! Pray for them, love them, speak truth to them, and then expect God to move into their life and transform them. In some cases, your faith in them will make the difference in their ability to accept the truth that God loves them, Jesus died for them, and the Holy Spirit is longing to live in them and bring them peace.

HEALING FOR THE HEART

THE TIME HAS COME TO TURN TO GOD
AND REASSERT OUR TRUST IN HIM FOR
THE HEALING OF AMERICA.

— RONALD REAGAN

There are many reasons for broken hearts and shattered dreams. Some are of our own making, and some are a consequence of the family and environment we were born into. But there isn't a person on the earth who hasn't been hurt, wounded, and broken by life in some way or another. Hurt and pain come with the territory; you live on this planet and you're going to have to deal with adversity. Why? Because the adversary of God, who happens to hate your guts, roams around on the earth trying to wreak havoc whenever and wherever he can.

Whether we have been hurt by our own sin or an attack of the enemy, God is a mender of broken hearts and a repairer of shattered dreams. He will not turn His back on our mess, no matter what the reason for it. No one knew this better than David.

The Lord is close to the brokenhearted and saves those who are crushed in spirit. A righteous man may have many troubles, but the Lord delivers him from them all; he protects all his bones, not one of them will be broken.
Psalms 34:18-19 NIV

David had experienced many troubles, some of his own making, some because of his enemies. But God was always faithful to him, and He will be faithful to you. If you are struggling with a broken heart, I encourage you to go to the Father and pour out your heart to Him. He wants to heal you and mend you; He wants you to be whole and happy.

If you want to be effective in your mission for the kingdom of God, you need to be whole. Give God your brokenness today. Let His healing hands restore you to the place of strength and joy that He has ordained for you.

JESUS IS THE LAMB

During the R.I.O.T. tour, I would sing this little song to myself to stay in an attitude of worship. Then one day I thought, "Hey, if it makes me worship, maybe it'll work for someone else."

JESUS IS THE LAMB
JESUS IS THE LAMB THAT WAS SLAIN
JESUS IS THE LAMB
JESUS IS THE LAMB THAT WAS SLAIN
GLORY, GLORY AND HONOR
GLORY AND HONOR AND POWER AND PRAISE
GLORY, GLORY AND HONOR
GLORY AND HONOR AND POWER AND PRAISE

'CAUSE OF EVERYTHING YOU'VE DONE FOR ME TODAY
IT'S THE EASIEST THING FOR ME TO STAND AND SAY
LORD, YOU KNOW I LOVE YOU
LOVE YOU FROM THE BOTTOM OF MY HEART
AND MAY I ADD I'D LOVE TO
TELL EVERYONE I KNOW JUST WHO YOU ARE

COUNTING EVERY TIME YOU'VE HEARD
MY LONESOME CRY
YOU'VE COMMITTED TO NEVER EVER PASS ME BY
LORD, YOU KNOW I'M THANKFUL

THANKFUL JUST TO KNOW THAT YOU ARE NEAR
MAY I ADD I'D LOVE TO
SING IT TO EVERY SOUL WHO WANTS TO HEAR

HEAVEN AND EARTH MUST NOW PROCLAIM
JESUS IS THE LAMB
GLORY TO GOD THE PEOPLE SAY
JESUS IS, JESUS IS THE LAMB
SENT FROM HEAVEN AND REJECTED
JESUS IS THE LAMB
CRUCIFIED AND RESURRECTED
JESUS IS THE LAMB

GLORY, GLORY AND HONOR
GLORY AND HONOR AND POWER AND PRAISE
GLORY, GLORY AND HONOR
GLORY AND HONOR AND POWER AND PRAISE

HOLY IS THE LAMB
HOLY IS THE LAMB THAT WAS SLAIN
HOLY IS THE LAMB
HOLY IS THE LAMB THAT WAS SLAIN

ETERNAL LIFE

FOR YOU KNOW THAT IT WAS NOT WITH PERISHABLE THINGS SUCH AS SILVER OR GOLD THAT YOU WERE REDEEMED FROM THE EMPTY WAY OF LIFE HANDED DOWN TO YOU FROM YOUR FOREFATHERS, BUT WITH THE PRECIOUS BLOOD OF CHRIST, A LAMB WITHOUT BLEMISH OR DEFECT.
— 1 PETER 1:18,19 NIV

The Passover, still celebrated in the Jewish religion today, marks the time when God "passed over" the firstborn of the Hebrews and killed the firstborn of the Egyptians, because Pharaoh had refused to free God's people. The Israelites were directed by Moses to kill a lamb and prepare it for eating without breaking a bone of its body. They were then to sprinkle the blood of the lamb on the doorposts of their homes so the Death Angel would pass by when he saw the blood sacrifice. (See Exodus 12.)

When Jesus came as the fulfillment of the Passover, most Jews did not recognize Him as the Lamb of God. But for those who believed in Him as the Messiah, His shed blood was placed on the doorposts of their hearts, protecting and cleansing them forever.

Many people today still do not comprehend the power in Jesus' blood. Scripture states that life itself is in the blood. (See Leviticus 17:14.) Many believe this to be a medical fact, but it is also a spiritual reality. The only way man can truly have eternal life is through the shed blood of Jesus.

Perhaps it has been some time since you actually thought about the price that was paid for your life. Maybe it is time to find someone this week and tell them about the One who loved them so much that He gave His life — shed His blood — for them. After all, it is your mission!

And he shewed me a pure river of water of life, clear as crystal, proceeding out of the throne of God and of the Lamb.

Revelation 22:1

DUTY

**THE HIGHEST LEVEL OF
MATURITY IS DUTY.**

— C. M. WARD

To protect themselves from hostile Indians, pioneer settlers built stockades around their settlements, each with a high pole. On top of these poles was an iron receptacle filled with flammable material. When Indians would come, the material was lighted as a signal. One day some of the settlers were surrounded by murderous Indians armed with poisoned arrows. When a brave youth climbed the pole to light the signal, poisoned arrows pierced his body, and he fell lifeless to the ground. Seeing the lighted fire, the nearby settlers came to the rescue. On a marker over this youth's grave were these words: "He saved others, Himself he could not save." This young man understood *duty*.

> *"He saved others," they said, "but he can't save himself! He's the king of Israel! Let him come down now from the cross, and we will believe in him."*

> *Matthew 27:42* NIV

Jesus did not want to die, but He understood duty.

Duty gets things done no matter how difficult the task may be. There will always be things in life that we do not want to do, but if we have a strong sense of duty — if we are mature — we will face them and trust God to see us through.

It is our duty to share the Gospel with the world. Every now and then, when I'm in a restaurant and God tells me the waiter is not saved, I have to remind myself that witnessing to people is not an option or a suggestion. It is my *duty!*

The great part about all this is, when I do my duty, obey God, and do what is right, I always stand back afterwards and wonder, "Why was I so uptight about this, anyway? What was the big deal?"

I've come to realize that the "big deal" is that God is growing me up into a mature man! So the next time you have the opportunity to share Jesus Christ, do your duty! Not only are you performing your mission, but you will be growing up in God.

HONOR

> THE SECRET OF MY SUCCESS? IT IS
> SIMPLE. IT IS FOUND IN THE BIBLE, "IN
> ALL THY WAYS ACKNOWLEDGE HIM AND
> HE SHALL DIRECT THY PATHS."
>
> — GEORGE WASHINGTON CARVER

There is an old Japanese custom that when someone saves your life, you belong to them. You must serve them for the remainder of your days. I do not know if a society can dictate such an order, but in theory it seems to present some interesting issues. What if someone saved your life, then treated your service as slavery and abused you? Custom would require that you stay, because they had been your savior.

The truth is, someone can save you and you can still choose not to honor him. But you cannot make someone the *lord* of your life without giving them *all* honor. If you have made Jesus your Lord, you have given Him your whole heart. You are now honoring Him with your heart and your mouth. (See Romans 15:6.) And you are honoring Him with your body. (See 1 Corinthians 6:20.) You are giving Him ALL OF YOU. That is the ultimate honor you can bestow upon anybody.

I am crucified with Christ: nevertheless I live; yet not I, but Christ liveth in me: and the life which I now live in the flesh I live by the faith of the Son of God, who loved me, and gave himself for me.

Galatians 2:20

Remember how Jesus began the Lord's Prayer? He began by honoring the very name of His Father God. If you have not been honoring God lately, begin this week. As soon as your alarm goes off in the morning, quietly begin to thank Him for the blessings in your life. Then throughout the day find three things in which to honor Him. If you are a servant of the Most High God, Master of the Universe, don't you think you should honor Him?

Give everyone what you owe him...if honor then honor.

Romans 13:7 NIV

THE COURTROOM

This was the sermon I preached on the R.I.O.T. tour every night before the altar call. Usually, I write story songs from other people's sermons. It's the first time since "The Champion" that I wrote one from my own.

IF TONIGHT YOU STOOD IN HEAVEN'S COURT
TO SEEK ETERNAL FAVOR
WOULD YOU FACE JESUS CHRIST AS JUDGE
OR WOULD YOU FACE HIM AS YOUR SAVIOR?

THERE ARE MANY WHO DON'T QUITE KNOW FOR SURE
WHAT THAT VERDICT WOULD BE IF EVER
SO LET'S IMAGINE FOR A MOMENT YOU'RE STANDING
    DEAD CENTER
IN THE COURTROOM OF FOREVER

SITTING BEFORE YOU IS A STRUCTURE
MASSIVE AND INTENSE
IT'S HERE YOUR FATE WILL BE DETERMINED
BEFORE THIS JUDGE'S BENCH

THEN A VOICE BOOMS, "THIS COURT'S NOW IN SESSION"
AND YOUR ADRENALINE STARTS TO RUSH
PEERING DOWN WITH EYES THAT SEE THROUGH
    YOUR SOUL
IS GOD THE FATHER; YOUR JUDGE

THEN OFF TO YOUR LEFT ACROSS THE ROOM
IS THE VIRTUAL SILHOUETTE OF SIN
STEPPING OUT OF THE SHADOWS OF CONDEMNATION
YOUR WORST NIGHTMARE WALKS IN

ON HIS FACE IS THE SMIRK OF EVIL INCARNATE
HIS MIND FIXED ON YOUR DESTRUCTION IN HELL
YOU'VE JUST BEEN INTRODUCED TO YOUR PROSECUTING
   ATTORNEY
NONE OTHER THAN SATAN HIMSELF

THE BIBLE SAYS HE'S THE ACCUSER OF THE BRETHREN
SO GUESS WHAT HE'S GONNA DO
HE'S GONNA ACCUSE YOU OF YOUR SINS
AND HE KNOWS THEM ALL
BOTH THE OLD ONES AND THE NEW

HE'S PREPARED HIS CASE FOR YEARS
NOW THE GOLDEN MOMENT IS HIS
SO IN ARROGANCE HE PRESENTS HIS CASE TO THE JUDGE
AND IT COMES OUT SOUNDING SOMETHING LIKE THIS

"GOD, YOU SEE THIS WORTHLESS PIECE OF TRASH
   OVER HERE?
THIS ONE IS A SINNER TO THE CORE
THIS ONE HAS COMMITTED ADULTERY, CURSED HIS
   NEIGHBOR, STOLEN MONEY
BEEN INTO DRUGS, ALCOHOL, AND EVEN MORE

"THIS HOPELESS WRETCH HAS EVEN SLANDERED FRIENDS
AND BY THAT GUILTY FACE THIS WHOLE COURTROOM
    CAN TELL
THAT TO A MORAL CERTAINTY AND BEYOND ANY
    REASONABLE DOUBT
THIS ONE DESERVES ETERNAL JUDGMENT IN HELL"

THE WORDS OF ACCUSATION STILL ECHO
YOUR EVERY SIN THROWN UP IN YOUR FACE
THEN GOD OPENS THE BOOK WHERE EVERY DEED IS
    RECORDED
AND REVIEWS YOUR RECORDS OF DISGRACE

GOD SAYS, "THE BOOK SAYS YOU DID THIS, THIS, AND THIS,
AND EVERYTHING YOU WERE ACCUSED OF TODAY
NOW, BEFORE I SENTENCE YOU TO HELL FOREVER
ARE THERE ANY LAST WORDS YOU HAVE TO SAY?"

NOW, IF IT'S TRUE YOU'RE STANDING THERE IN THE
    COURTROOM OF ETERNITY
WITH GOD TO YOUR FRONT AND SATAN THE
    PROSECUTOR TO YOUR LEFT
THERE'S ONE REMAINING ETERNAL TRUTH, ONE THAT'S
    CRUCIAL TO REMEMBER
ONE YOU SHOULD NEVER, EVER, EVER FORGET.

THAT ON THE OTHER SIDE OF THE COURTROOM
I SAID, ON THE OTHER SIDE OF THE COURTROOM
YOU AIN'T HEARING ME TONIGHT
I SAID, ON THE OTHER SIDE OF THE COURTROOM

Is the one and only Son of God
Revealed in time and space
And He's your Defense Attorney
Who's never lost a case

It's not Buddha, Mohammed or Krishna
Or any others who succumb to death
Ladies and gentlemen, on the other side of the
courtroom
Is Jesus Christ of Nazareth

Then Jesus jumps up, says, "Wait a minute, Judge
Now I've got something to say
May I remind You that on a cross 2,000 years ago
I washed his sins away

"I was crucified, I died, they put Me in a tomb
But long about the midnight hour
The power of God hit Me and I walked out of
that grave
Alive and well with resurrection power"

Then the devil said, "It's in the book, it's written
in the book
Check the book," and God said, "OK"
Then He takes the book out, lays it open and says
"Now, we'll see what this book has to say"

HE TURNS TO THE FIRST PAGE, THE SECOND PAGE, THE
THIRD
BY THE FOURTH, THE DEVIL SEEMS SHOOK
GOD CLOSES IT AND SAYS, "THE BLOOD OF JESUS MUST
HAVE WORKED
'CAUSE THERE IS ABSOLUTELY NOTHING IN THIS BOOK"

THE DEVIL SAYS, "NOW, WAIT A MINUTE, CHECK THAT
BOOK AGAIN
ALL HIS SINS ARE WRITTEN DOWN, THEY'RE ALL RIGHT
THERE"
GOD SAID, "DEVIL, MAYBE YOU'RE MISTAKEN ALL
TOGETHER
MAYBE IT'S THIS OTHER BOOK DOWN HERE"

THE DEVIL CRIES, "NO! NOT THAT BOOK,
NOT THAT ONE"
GOD SAID, "DEVIL, WHY YOU SO UPTIGHT?"
GOD GETS THE BOOK DOWN, THE DUST FLIES
AND ON THE COVER IT SAYS
THE LAMB'S BOOK OF LIFE

IS YOUR NAME IN THAT BOOK?
IS YOUR NAME IN THAT BOOK?
IS YOUR NAME IN THAT BOOK FOR SURE?

IF YOU'VE BEEN FORGIVEN
AND YOUR NAME IS WRITTEN
THEN LIFT YOUR HANDS, PRAISE THE LORD

YES, MY NAME'S IN THAT BOOK
YES, MY NAME'S IN THAT BOOK
YES, MY NAME'S IN THAT BOOK TONIGHT
I'VE BEEN FORGIVEN
AND I KNOW MY NAME IS WRITTEN
IN THE LAMB'S BOOK OF LIFE
IN THE LAMB'S BOOK OF LIFE

THIS COURT IS ADJOURNED

HERE COMES THE JUDGE

THERE IS ONE GREAT GOD AND POWER THAT HATH MADE THE WORLD AND ALL THINGS THEREIN, TO WHOM YOU AND I AND ALL PEOPLE OWE THEIR BEING AND WELL-BEING, AND TO WHOM YOU AND I MUST ONE DAY GIVE AN ACCOUNT, FOR ALL THAT WE DO IN THE WORLD.

— WILLIAM PENN

The highest court of the United States is the Supreme Court. It consists of the chief justice and eight associate justices, all appointed by the president and confirmed by the Senate. These nine judges decide the legal issues for each case presented to them. Although the system is not perfect, it is the best system in the world.

When you present your case before the judges of this land, they consider all the evidence available to them. They can be swayed or misled by circumstances, faulty documentation, or an attorney's charismatic personality. Even though they may have years of experience on the bench, they are still human. No matter how wise or insightful, they can make mistakes.

In the courtroom of the universe there is but one judge, God Himself, the Righteous Judge. He is the only One wise enough to judge fairly in every circumstance. The Word of God tells us that man looks on the outward appearances — the things that are seen, easily observed, or readily available — but God looks on the heart. (See 2 Corinthians 10:7.)

When we stand before the Righteous Judge there is nothing hidden. There can be no twisting of facts, no spin on the truth, and no circumstantial evidence taken into consideration. He sees the intents of our heart — good or bad.

You might want to do a heart checkup this week. Make sure that nothing is standing between you and God. Then you will not be hindered in any way from completing your mission.

> *Who shall lay any thing to the charge of God's elect? It is God that justifieth.*
> *Romans 8:33*

THE PROSECUTING ATTORNEY

THERE IS AN OLD LAWYER JOKE THAT GOES LIKE THIS: QUESTION: "HOW DO YOU TELL IF A LAWYER IS LYING?" ANSWER: "HIS LIPS ARE MOVING."

I would like to believe that in most cases this is the exception, not the rule. However, in one case I am absolutely certain the accusing attorney is, was, and always will be the biggest liar on the face of the earth. As a matter of fact, he is the father of lies (see John 8:44), and the truth is not in him (see 1 John 2:4).

The one who stands against you in the courtroom of eternity is the greatest liar of all time. He twists every fact about your life. He embellishes and magnifies every mistake you have ever made. He blows up your sins to the point that even you might be tempted to believe the lies. His aim is to steal your eternal home, kill your reputation, and destroy you before the court.

For we wrestle not against flesh and blood, but against principalities, against powers, against the rulers of the darkness of this world, against spiritual wickedness in high places.

Ephesians 6:12

Satan, the prosecutor, can say whatever he likes about you to your Father God, but to no avail. You have been washed in the blood of Jesus, and all you need to do is remind him of your salvation and your total commitment to the Lord.

And they overcame him by the blood of the Lamb, and by the word of their testimony; and they loved not their lives unto the death.

Revelation 12:11

Begin to win your case today! First, don't give the prosecutor any ammunition by sinning, and if you do sin, run immediately to 1 John 1:9, be forgiven and cleansed, and get back on track with the Lord. Then, send your prosecutor into a tail spin by telling your salvation testimony to someone and bringing them into the kingdom!

THE DEFENSE ATTORNEY

THE MAN WHO REPRESENTS HIMSELF HAS A FOOL FOR A CLIENT.

— ANONYMOUS

You have the ultimate legal counsel: Jesus Christ. Each morning He stands ready and waiting to plead your case before the Father and give you the best advice available.

Now Jesus happens to know the prosecuting attorney personally — they met before time began. In fact, there was one particular run-in with the prosecutor that Jesus never wants us to forget. (See Luke 4:1-13.) The prosecutor tried his lying tactics on Jesus, making promises and attaching some provisions that could have cost Him everything. But Jesus was too smart for him and sent him packing! And He knows how to deal with him on your behalf right now.

Most attorneys can only represent their clients, but Jesus actually removes your guilt and your shame — if you'll let Him. This is very important, because the prosecutor is out there saying a lot of rotten things about you and spreading all kinds of vicious rumor. You can come under terrible condo-bondo (condemnation and bondage) if you don't let Jesus heal you and clean you up.

It is time to stop him in his tracks!

> *My little children, these things write I unto you, that ye sin not. And if any man sin, we have an advocate with the Father, Jesus Christ the righteous: And he is the propitiation for our sin: and not for ours only, but also for the sins of the whole world.*
>
> *1 John 2:1-2*

Get yourself a lawyer! Begin to see yourself forgiven and protected by your defense attorney, Jesus Christ. Then go out and tell your family, friends, and neighbors that you know a great attorney, and everyone needs a great attorney!

THE WITNESSES

> LET ALL THE NATIONS BE GATHERED
> TOGETHER, AND LET THE PEOPLE BE
> ASSEMBLED: WHO AMONG THEM CAN
> DECLARE THIS, AND SHEW US FORMER
> THINGS? LET THEM BRING FORTH
> THEIR WITNESSES, THAT THEY MAY
> BE JUSTIFIED: OR LET THEM HEAR,
> AND SAY, IT IS TRUTH.
> — *ISAIAH 43:9*

When you are going to trial a very important part of your defense will be a list of witnesses.

Anyone who can say anything good about you, substantiate your claim, or give testimony to your good character will be called.

You can only be a witness if you have something to tell.

Paul tells us in Hebrews 12:1 that we are surrounded by a great cloud of witnesses. I believe they are those who have testimonies, those who have endured and now sit in the grandstands of heaven cheering us on. Each time the prosecutor tries to get us down, I believe there is a testimony service going on in heaven! In the Spirit today, can you hear them encouraging you?

"You can make it!" David calls. "I failed miserably, but God forgave me, and I am here to testify about His incredible mercies — which are new *every* morning, by the way."

"You go, girl!" cries Queen Esther. "I overcame my fear of what might happen to me if I asked the king to spare my people, because God was right there with me all the way. And I'm here to testify that He will be with you too."

"Don't give up!" Paul shouts. "Silas and I were beaten, put in the darkest dungeon of a prison, and put in stocks. But we are witnesses today that when we began praising God, He showed up, showed off, and set us free! Not only that, He saved the jailer and his family!"

I tell you, today you've got your witnesses, a grandstand full of them who are cheering you on. So if you haven't started — or you've stopped — don't you think it's time to go out and be a witness for Jesus yourself! If you don't feel you've got much to tell now, believe me, in a few days of testifying, you will!

SURF MISSION

When I was growing up, I used to watch the surfers in the beach party movies. After awhile it was really obvious that a surfer could be highly skilled, but if the waves weren't good, the surfing wasn't good. Our Mission 3:16 is the same way. We can have all the witnessing techniques down, hold huge crusades, and preach our hearts out, but if the Holy Spirit doesn't show up, nothing happens. The good news is, when we do what the Holy Spirit and the Word tell us to do, He always shows up! Like a mighty tidal wave, He will sweep in and gather all the lost souls into His kingdom.

SURFING USA

**PERSISTENCE AND A POSITIVE ATTITUDE
ARE NECESSARY INGREDIENTS FOR
ANY SUCCESSFUL VENTURE.**
— LAURA INGLES WILDER

The 1960s saw the rise of a unique music message as the Beach Boys started the surfing music craze. The sound grew and took over the music charts from coast to coast, even in remote places that had never seen a surfer.

The duo, Jan and Dean, released their hit "Surf City" in the mid '60s. But not long after their rise to stardom, a near fatal car crash threatened the life of Dean. The prognosis for his recovery was not promising. But against the odds, Dean began to walk again and regain a normal life. For months he could not speak, and when his speech returned it was slurred and nearly impossible to understand.

Before the accident, Jan and Dean had signed a contract to do a concert with the Beach Boys. Since Dean could not speak clearly, the duo decided to sing softly while playing their recording loudly, thus drowning out the slurs in Dean's vocals. During the concert an electrical problem occurred and the recording stopped. The crowd booed and jeered as they heard the real Dean singing.

Taking their cause, one of the Beach Boys came on stage to the microphone. He admonished the audience and reintroduced Jan and Dean, who would now have to sing without any background coverup. This time they were graciously received. Dean's story is one of extraordinary determination and perseverance. Too often we are tempted to give up when trials come and things get rough.

You may have tried to go on, to get up and share again, but you were laughed down or mocked and ridiculed. Remind yourself every day that you are victorious and Jesus is on your side. There is not one circumstance He cannot help you overcome.

> ***I can do everything through him who gives me strength.***
>
> **Philippians 4:13** NIV

SILVER SURFER

> **MANY PEOPLE MISTAKE OUR WORK**
> **FOR OUR VOCATION.**
> **OUR VOCATION IS THE LOVE OF JESUS.**
> — **MOTHER TERESA**

Along with the glut of super heroes to emerge in comic book form was a lesser-known interplanetary character known as the Silver Surfer. His mission was to find his woman who had mysteriously disappeared. He traveled on a surf board that was much like the hoverboard used by Michael J. Fox in the *Back to the Future* movies.

Like his counterparts, Superman, Batman, The Green Hornet, and Spider Man, the Silver Surfer's adventures led him to fight a hoard of bad guys as he searched the earth for his lost love. He was driven by the desire to be reunited with the only woman he had ever loved.

In some ways, Jesus is on that same mission today. The Church is the Bride of Christ, but many of us have become so caught up in the things of this world that we have been drawn away from Him by the lusts of our own flesh and the pull of this world.

Are you Jesus' missing Bride? If you have drawn away from Him, come back today! Run into the loving arms of your Savior. Give yourself to Him once again.

> *Seek the Lord while he may be found; call on him while he is near.*
>
> Isaiah 55:6 NIV

You will never be content until you have totally surrendered to Jesus and are truly acting like His Bride. You see, when we act like the Bride of Christ, He can use us to save those who are lost. He is using His Bride to complete His Body!

The Bride reflects the glory of the Bridegroom, which is His love for her. She radiates His love to everyone around her. Because He has shown her such compassion and mercy, she imparts His compassion and mercy to others. The wisdom and truth that He has given her, she freely gives to all who are in need.

When you act like Jesus' Bride, you bring Him to the world — Mission 3:16!

MURF THE SURF

> GOD IS GOING TO REVEAL TO US THINGS
> HE NEVER REVEALED BEFORE IF WE PUT
> OUR HANDS IN HIS.
>
> — GEORGE WASHINGTON CARVER

Jack Roland Murphy was a leader in the "surfing set" in Miami Beach, Florida. He manufactured surfboards, and with his skills on the waves earned the name "Murf the Surf." But Murf had a plan to do more than surf.

On October 29, 1964, Murf robbed the American Museum of Natural History and stole a collection of precious gems. His mission was executed perfectly. He and his partner overcame every security device, and it seemed their plan was foolproof.

Murf's next plan was to jet off to some sunshine and sparkling beaches where he could find high surf and pretty girls, but God had another plan for this surfer. Just two days after the robbery, the F.B.I. kicked in the door of Murf's penthouse and hauled him off to jail.

In and out of jails and often shackled like an animal, Murf still continued to plan, but nothing was producing. Then God revealed His plan. He sent Max Jones, Prison Chaplain, into Murf's world. At first, the plan of salvation seemed too simple to Murf. He was used to his own intricate plans — like the one that had landed him in jail! Finally the message got through and Murf traded his plans for the plan of God.

On December 20, 1985, after seventeen years in prison, Murf finally walked out, a free man. He was armed with a new plan — a mission for God.

> *"For I know the plans I have for you," declares the Lord, "plans to prosper you and not to harm you, plans to give you hope and a future. Then you will call upon me and come and pray to me, and I will listen to you. You will seek me and find me when you seek me with all your heart."*
>
> *Jeremiah 29:11-13* NIV

Do you need to trade your plans for the plan of God? Believe me — and learn from Murf the Surf — it is the best way!

DO I DO?

This actually was a children's song I wrote ten years ago, a song about faith and trust that a child could understand. All I needed was a down-home Cajun treatment to bring it to life.

Do I Do
Yes, I say
Trust in You, Lord
All the way
Do I Do
Yes, I say
Trust in You
All the way

Daniel was in trouble in the lions' den
But he knew what prayer was all about
Daniel trusted God and he got out again
He didn't doubt, he didn't doubt

Moses told the pharaoh back in Egypt land
God said, "Pharaoh, let My people go"
After many plagues, people fled and then
They headed for the promised land

EVERYTHING I AM
EVERYTHING I'LL BE
EVERYTHING I'LL DO
YOU DECIDE FOR ME

PETER SAW THE MASTER WALKING ON THE SEA
PETER SAID, "CAN I COME OUT TO YOU?"
JESUS TOLD HIM, "PETER, I CAN MAKE IT BE
IF ALL YOU DO IS TRUST IN ME"

A MATTER OF TRUST

IN LONG EXPERIENCE I FIND THAT A MAN WHO TRUSTS NOBODY IS APT TO BE A MAN NOBODY TRUSTS.

— HAROLD MACMILLAN

Today it is nearly impossible to trust anyone. We have been misled and lied to by so many who once had our trust, both privately and publicly. Many occupations that once commanded trust have now become suspect: teachers have failed us, law officers have shown themselves to be all too human, and elected officials have taken unfair advantage of their power and position.

And no one trusts us either! The companies we work for hire us and then install cameras to monitor our actions. Parents wire their homes to spy on their children's caregivers. One major department store chain requires its female workers to carry clear plastic handbags so stolen merchandise cannot walk out the door with them.

The worst part is, half the time I don't trust myself! Like Paul in Romans 7:15, I say and do things I don't want to say and do, and the things I do want to say and do, I don't say and do. So what do we do? (It really does make sense, trust me...)

We can trust God first, then He will show us who to trust and when. It is impossible for God to lie. (See Hebrews 6:18.) He has only good plans for us. (See Jeremiah 29:11.) And He does not change — say one thing and do another. (See Malachi 3:6.)

When I was recording my album of hymns, I was struck by the fact that certain ones confirmed how much I trusted Jesus for everything in life: "What a Friend We Have in Jesus," "Leaning on the Everlasting Arms," and "'Tis So Sweet to Trust in Jesus." If you meditate on the words, listen to them, and begin to praise and worship God with them, before you know it, you will be trusting God more and more.

And let's face it, if you don't trust God, you'll never fulfill the mission He's given you, because you cannot do it without Him!

YES, LORD, YES

HEAVENLY FATHER, MAY ALL REVERE
THEE, AND BECOME THY DUTIFUL
CHILDREN AND FAITHFUL SUBJECTS.
— BENJAMIN FRANKLIN

During Ronald Reagan's presidency, the First Lady, Nancy Reagan, began her campaign against drugs. The slogan, "Just Say No," is still used today. No is usually one of the first words a baby will say. They repeat what they often hear. The word no is ingrained in us from childhood.

Yes is a word we learn much later. A dear friend of mine was taught by her southern parents to say, "Yes, ma'am," and "Yes, sir," whenever she was given a command. But today we hear no, more than yes. We have almost forgotten yes, the word of surrender.

In order to receive all God has for us, we must learn to say yes to Him. One of the most precious songs to come out of the Church is a reminder of that word of surrender. "Yes Lord, Yes, Lord, Yes, Lord, Yes, Yes, Yes."

"Yes" means I will, I do, I agree. One church I attended even placed the words over the doors of each

church exit, "Yes, Lord." We were constantly remind-
ed to commit our will to the will of God for our lives.

It is time for the Church of the living God to come
back to the condition of YES. You may have given your
life to God, but still have difficulty in saying yes to His
will, or yes to His way. Speak to your soul in the words
of the familiar old chorus, "I say yes, Lord, yes. From
the bottom of my heart, from the depths of my soul,
Yes, Lord, completely yes. My soul says yes."

*For no matter how many promises God
has made, they are "Yes" in Christ. And so
through him the "Amen" is spoken by us to
the glory of God.*

2 Corinthians 1:20 NIV

GOD'S YES MAN

IF ALL THE SONS AND DAUGHTERS OF THE CHURCH WOULD KNOW HOW TO BE TIRELESS MISSIONARIES OF THE GOSPEL, A NEW AND FLOWERING OF HOLINESS AND RENEWAL WOULD SPRING UP IN THIS WORLD THAT THIRSTS FOR LOVE AND FOR TRUTH.

— POPE JOHN PAUL I

When someone refers to another as a "Yes Man," they usually mean someone who is always agreeing no matter what they really believe. A "Yes Man" most often will say yes to your face, then behind your back they do whatever they think is best. A "Yes Man" is usually not respected by his co-workers, because he is always trying to gain favor with his "yes attitude." But God's "yes man" is simply always saying yes to God.

Jesus gave us many illustrations of God's "yes man": the good Samaritan in Luke 10:29-37, who showed mercy to the man who had been left for dead on the road; the "good and faithful" servants in Matthew 25:14-30, who took the talents their master had given them and multiplied them; and the "sheep" in Matthew 25:32-40, who treated everyone they met as though they were Jesus Himself — feeding the hungry, clothing the naked, visiting the sick and those in prison.

> *But he that is greatest among you shall be your servant. And whosoever shall exalt himself shall be abased; and he that shall humble himself shall be exalted.*
>
> *Matthew 23:11-12*

Abraham said yes to God even when he thought he might have to sacrifice his precious son. Noah said yes to God even though building a boat brought him ridicule. Moses said yes to God and went back to Egypt to free his people from Pharaoh even though he was wanted for murder. Daniel said yes to God by continuing to pray, even over the threat of a lions' den. The three Hebrew children said yes to God and no to Nebuchadnezzar though it meant walking into a fiery furnace.

Have you said yes to God for your life? Your surrender and submission to Him will bring about the yes you need to carry out your mission!

WE ARE NOT ASHAMED

After seeing the over one-million-man Promise Keepers march on Washington, this song just forced itself to the surface. If you picture that special day in your mind while this song is playing, you'll understand the full meaning of what happened that day.

SOME PEOPLE WONDER WHY WE TAKE THE CHANCES
    THAT WE DO
TO BRING THE WORD OF GOD INTO THE WORKPLACE
    AND THE SCHOOLS
WE'RE LOOKED UPON AS OUTCASTS
FANATICS THEY MAY SAY
SO WHY THEN DO WE STILL PERSIST
TO SHARE OUR FAITH THIS WAY?
IT'S BECAUSE…

WE ARE NOT ASHAMED OF THE GOSPEL OF JESUS CHRIST
FOR IT IS THE WORD OF GOD TO EVERY NATION
WE ARE NOT ASHAMED OF THE GOSPEL OF JESUS CHRIST
FOR IT IS THE POWER OF SALVATION

For those of you who fight the wars
Against our nation's sins
Heroes who give so much more than is required
    of them
For those of you who paid a price
Beyond what words can say
Remember that you're not alone
With the cross you bear each day

Jesus Christ was wounded, too
With wounds deeper than ours
That's why no child of God
Should be embarrassed by their scars
So lift up your head
You weary saint
Be strong in Jesus' name
The battle's won, the victory's ours
Let's stand up and proclaim…

That it's the Gospel that saved us
And the Gospel that raised us
And the Gospel that gave us everlasting life

MARCHING AND MOVING

WE'RE MARCHING AND MOVING,
ONWARD AND UPWARD,
THE KINGDOM OF GOD IS ON
A FORCEFUL ADVANCE.
WE ARE TAKING DOMINION
OVER THE DARKNESS,
TEARING DOWN THE WALLS
OF THE ENEMIES HANDS.

— GARY OLIVER

On Sunday, July 20, 1776, General George Washington was preparing his troops to advance against the British. The cause of freedom had finally come to a head and the army was prepared to fight for it. On that day, General Washington first encouraged the soldiers to observe the day and attend church services, but told them to be ready to take immediate action if necessary. He admonished his troops:

THE FATE OF UNBORN MILLIONS WILL NOW DEPEND, UNDER GOD, ON THE COURAGE OF THIS ARMY. OUR CRUEL AND UNRELENTING ENEMY LEAVES US ONLY THE CHOICE OF BRAVE RESISTANCE, OR THE MOST ABJECT SUBMISSION.

WE HAVE THEREFORE TO RESOLVE TO CONQUER OR DIE.

The battle is once again raging in America. Our religious freedoms are being threatened. Movies, television, magazines, newspapers, and even the educational channels on TV mock religious values and promote humanistic thinking. As a result, immoral thinking and behavior is at an all-time high. Some basic religious freedoms, such as prayer in public schools, have already been legislated away. It is time to stand up and put God in America again!

Are you ready to march and move, unashamed, armed with the Gospel of Jesus Christ? You must be ready at a moment's notice to march into the enemy's camp and take back what has been stolen from you. Arm yourself with the Word of God and the power of the Spirit. Then go forth to declare the name of Jesus in your neighborhood, your school, your city, and your country.

When each of us carries out our Mission 3:16, America will be called a Christian nation once more.

HOLY BOLDNESS

IF YOU DON'T STAND FOR SOMETHING, YOU WILL FALL FOR ANYTHING.

— UNKNOWN

The central character of the first *Star Trek* television series and movies was Captain James T. Kirk. Every episode would begin with his statement, "...to boldly go were no man has gone before." Kirk was a pioneer, an adventurer, and a trained explorer with an experienced crew and an amazing armed vehicle called the *Starship Enterprise*. To all of us who watched the series and saw the movies later, he was a true hero. He was honest, he was just, he was wise, and he was strong. But most of all, he had that boldness, a fearlessness that did the right thing no matter what the consequences.

It was easy for Captain Kirk, because he read the script and knew the ending when he started! But what about us? How can we face down the enemy of intimidation every time we are to tell someone about Jesus?

Now, Lord, consider their threats and enable your servants to speak your word with great boldness. After they prayed, the place where they were meeting was shaken. And they were all filled with the Holy Spirit and spoke the word of God boldly.

Acts 4:29,31 NIV

When you come face to face with the enemy of your soul, you cannot run in fear. You must boldly face him. By drawing near to God, you engage your shield of faith and aggressively move in on the enemy with your sword, the Word of God. (See Ephesians 6.) It is not a fearful task if you *know* the Source of your strength and the Power who is behind you.

Then you can march in with a boldness only the Holy Spirit can give and tell a lost and dying world that they can be saved. As you are endued with power from on high, you will boldly proclaim to them, "Jesus is Lord, and He wants to save, heal, and deliver you right now!"

And by the way, if you read your script, it says that Satan cannot stop your mission!

FEARLESS FANATICS

WHEN I LEFT THE HOUSE OF BONDAGE
I LEFT EVERYTHING BEHIND. I WANTED
TO KEEP NOTHING OF EGYPT ON ME,
AND SO I WENT TO THE LORD AND
ASKED HIM TO GIVE ME A NEW NAME....
I SET UP MY BANNER, AND THEN I SING,
AND THEN FOLKS ALWAYS COMES UP
'ROUND ME, AND THEN...
I TELLS THEM ABOUT JESUS.
— SOJOURNER TRUTH (A FREED SLAVE)

When I think of fearless fanatics, two examples in Scripture jump out at me: one a man, the other a woman. Since my mother always said, "Ladies first," I will tell you about Queen Esther. When the evil Haman petitioned the king to issue an edict that allowed for the killing of all the Jews in the kingdom, Queen Esther, being a Jew, was in the position to save her people. God had placed her in the kingdom for "such a time as this" (Esther 4:14).

After fasting and praying, she boldly proclaimed, "If I perish, I perish," and asked to see the king. Humbling herself before him, she requested protection for her people. The king issued a counterorder which allowed the Jews to arm and protect themselves against the previously ordered attack. Because of Esther's fearless faith, her people were saved.

John the Baptist was also a fearless fanatic. He was a child born of a promise to aging parents. (See Luke 1.) He was a Nazarene and never cut his hair or touched strong drink. (See Luke 1:15.) He knew the fine art of practicing self-denial. He loved solitude and communicating with God in the desert. He dressed simply, wearing cloth woven from camel's hair, and had a strange diet. (See Matthew 3:4.)

John was a simple man in every way in the natural, but he was a radical for God. He was the one God chose to declare that Jesus was the Son of God, the Messiah, and he was executed for his stand for righteousness. Jesus grieved when he heard of John's death, and said that John was the greatest of all the prophets of Israel.

Do something today to be a fearless fanatic for Jesus, and you will be in good company!

THE PRAYER ANTHEM

I always had trouble singing that long ballad version of The Lord's Prayer that we all know. I just said to myself, "Why doesn't somebody write one that's easy enough, so simple people like me can sing?"

> OUR FATHER WHICH ART IN HEAVEN
> HALLOWED BE THY NAME
> THY KINGDOM COME
> THY WILL BE DONE
> ON EARTH AS IT IS IN HEAVEN
>
> AND GIVE TO US
> OUR DAILY BREAD
> AND FORGIVE US OUR DEBTS
> AS WE FORGIVE OUR DEBTORS
>
> LEAD US NOT INTO
> TEMPTATION
> BUT DELIVER US
> DELIVER US FROM EVIL

THINE IS THE KINGDOM

THINE IS THE POWER

THINE IS THE GLORY

FOREVER AND EVER AND EVER AND EVER

THY KINGDOM COME

THY WILL BE DONE

ON EARTH AS IT IS IN HEAVEN

OUR FATHER

IT IS A WISE FATHER THAT KNOWS HIS OWN CHILD.

— WILLIAM SHAKESPEARE

It is a challenge for many today to relate to a father, since many family units are without one living in the home. That makes it much more difficult for people to understand the concept of a Father God. Many have never known the love and care of a father. Others have known only abuse or neglect from their father.

Satan has worked tirelessly to destroy the family unit. In doing so he has muddied the thinking of young minds about fatherhood. Satan hates the Father, and he wants all men, women, boys, and girls to hate the whole idea of a father. Gone are the days of *Leave It to Beaver*, where Ward came home and handled the difficult character issues facing Beaver and Wally, then disciplined them firmly but affectionately.

Today we have Homer Simpson and Tim (The Tool Man) Taylor, who act like morons most of the time and incite little or no respect from their wives and children. Add most of society's personal experiences with their fathers — or lack of fathering — and we have a huge void in the family structure.

Carman

Deezer D. Shooting of "Courtroom" video.

Author signing 96 R.I.O.T. Tour.

Another R.I.O.T. bookstore signing.

Carman with Ann Marie who was his personal trainer at a Nashville Heath Club.

Stephen Yake, Carman, and Sigmund Johns, the choreographer and lead dancer, watching a play-back of the Slam Video from Mission 3:16.

Larry and Frances Jones of Feed the Children outside one of the R.I.O.T. Centers in Houston, Texas.

Signing an autograph for a fan at Planet Hollywood in Nashville.

Carman on location in Ireland filming Prayer Anthem segment for the Mission 3:16 video.

Jerry Reed of Smokey and the Bandit fame hanging out with Carman at a Baptist Hospital. (Carman was very excited to meet him!)

Carman, Tony Orlando, and Stephen Yake during the shooting of the Mission 3:16 video on location in Nashville.

Country Western singer Ricky Skaggs at the R.I.O.T. Release Party in Nashville.

Visiting friends backstage at the Thunderdome in Tampa/St. Petersburg R.I.O.T. Tour.

Willie Aames AKA Bibleman, Mark Wayne, Carman, and Brian Lemmons, at Planet Hollywood in Nashville. Willie, who once played Tommy Bradford on Eight is Enough, was giving a Bibleman costume for Planet Hollywood to display. Mark and Brian once danced for Carman and now travel with Bibleman.

We cannot undo society or our own personal father issues, but God can. Through Jesus, we can know the REAL FATHER. He heals us and restores us and makes up for anything we missed from our natural fathers, which will provide the foundation we need to fulfill our mission.

Remember, the Father wants all the children He can get! That's why He put a desire in you to bring more children into His kingdom. It is your mission to share with others about our Father, the One who will never leave nor forsake us, the One who gives us peace in the midst of the storm, and the One who has prepared a glorious eternity for all who are committed to Him.

For ye have not received the spirit of bondage again to fear; but ye have received the Spirit of adoption, whereby we cry, Abba, Father.

Romans 8:15

THY WILL BE DONE

WE HAVE TO BELIEVE IN FREE WILL.
WE'VE GOT NO CHOICE.
— ISAAC BASHEVIS SINGER

I love that quote! It declares the truth in an ironic fashion: We have to choose. Everything we do involves a choice. We might say that we hold at least 51 percent of the stock in our lives. We always cast the deciding vote on where to go and what to do and what to say — and God holds no one but us responsible for those choices.

Needless to say, the will is a powerful instrument. It's interesting to me that God would give us such a wonderful gift of choice and then ask us to give it back to Him, surrendering our human will to His divine will. But He is God. He knows best. And He wants His children to have the best at all times and in all situations. So He says, "Choose My way. Choose life!"

Jesus is our supreme example of surrendering our will. Every time He was faced with temptation, He chose to obey His heavenly Father. Ultimately, He chose to sacrifice His life to provide eternal life for you and me.

I remember when I knew it was time to surrender a part of my ministry to God in a big way. I felt the Lord leading me not to charge for our concerts, but to take love offerings instead. I was used to knowing what the expenses were and what my budgeted income would be. This was a giant leap of faith for me. But God kept leading me to open the doors free of charge so that families could come and bring their unsaved friends, neighbors, and loved ones. He said, "Freely you have received; now freely give."

When I obeyed, when I surrendered my way to Him, I found out God's will always produces better results than mine! My ministry began to grow dramatically and I discovered that although surrender is not easy, we walk in greater freedom and a deeper love for our Father God when we do things His way. What do you need to surrender today?

If you are willing and obedient, you will eat the best from the land.

Isaiah 1:19 NIV

GIVE US

> WHEN WE TAKE OUR MEALS, THERE IS
> THE GRACE. WHEN I TAKE A DRAUGHT
> OF WATER, I ALWAYS PAUSE...TO LIFT UP
> MY HEART TO GOD IN THANKS AND
> PRAYER FOR THE WATER OF LIFE.
> WHENEVER I [SEND] A LETTER...I SEND A
> PETITION ALONG WITH IT, FOR GOD'S
> BLESSING UPON ITS MISSION AND UPON
> THE PERSON TO WHOM IT IS SENT.
>
> — STONEWALL JACKSON

When Jesus began to pray He started by honoring His Father and glorifying His name. He surrendered His will to God and had a time of communion with Him before He ever asked for a thing. Today we might consider that to be "sucking up," but that is not at all what Jesus was doing. It is good to honor the one from whom you are requesting something, especially God. It's simply praise and worship, when you praise Him for all the great things He has done and is doing for you, and worship Him for all He is to you.

We need to be assured of God's love for us and "connect" with Him in order to ask Him for anything in faith. If we are "disconnected" or feeling guilty or intimidated at all about asking Him for things, chances are He won't respond, because the Bible tells us it is impossible to please God without faith, and He doesn't do anything apart from faith.

> *But without faith it is impossible to please him: for he that cometh to God must believe that he is, and that he is a rewarder of them that diligently seek him.*
>
> *Hebrews 11:6*

If I find myself feeling guilty or uncomfortable asking God for things, I just start praising Him and ask Him to show me what the problem is. I want to approach Him with confidence and faith, the way Jesus did when He was on earth. When Jesus began asking the Father for things, He asked for quite a bit, and I don't think He was feeling guilty about it either!

God wants us to ask freely and in faith, because that is how He helps us to accomplish the mission He's given us. What do you need from Him today? Ask Him!

FORGIVE US

TO ERR IS HUMAN, TO FORGIVE DIVINE.
— ALEXANDER POPE

When Jesus gave us the Lord's Prayer, He included forgiveness. He had lived a blameless life and had nothing to be forgiven for, but one thing Jesus did do was to forgive others and ask the Father to forgive them too. We need to continually seek God's forgiveness. We are not only to ask and receive forgiveness for our own sins, but we are to forgive others and ask God to forgive them.

> *And when you stand praying, if you hold anything against anyone, forgive him, so that your Father in heaven may forgive you your sins.*
>
> *Mark 11:25 NIV*

How many times have we prayed with an "attitude"? You know, those times when we mean, "Oh God, help so-and-so. You know that she is a real liar and she lied on me again this week. Get her good, God. She is a child of Satan and needs to be stopped." Or, "God, I just release You now to go and deal with my friend so-and-so. You know that he is a dirty rotten devil and has been messing up for a long time now. I can't stand being around him. God, he's hurt me too many times. You just have to deal with him."

> **HE, WHO CANNOT FORGIVE A TRESPASS OF MALICE TO HIS ENEMY, HAS NEVER TASTED THE MOST SUBLIME ENJOYMENT OF LOVE.**
> **— JOHANN KASPER LAVATER**

Instead of taking someone else's sins to God, forgive them and then ask God to forgive them! Your forgiving attitude will release the person to God so He can deal with them. It will also clear your relationship with God so that you can repent and receive forgiveness for yourself. The best part of all of this is, when your relationship with God is on track, you will know His will for your life and receive His strength to carry out your mission.

Let the Holy Ghost's light "x-ray" your heart right now! Don't waste a moment being unforgiven or unforgiving.

LEAD US

> **THE PUREST FORM OF LEADERSHIP IS INFLUENCE THROUGH INSPIRATION.**
> — MYLES MUNROE

When Jesus asked His Father God to lead us, He knew that human beings, for the most part, needed leadership. Scripture often refers to us as sheep, and by their very nature sheep require leading. Sheep need to be led to quiet places of peace. They need protection from wild beasts, and when they are sick with sores, they need their shepherd to medicate them with the healing oil he carries. If sheep are not led, they will run all over the countryside. They will fall into ravines, get stuck in bramble bushes, or become food for some animal.

As human beings, we are a little less cooperative than real sheep. We don't want anyone telling us what to do. Generally we do not want to submit to anyone, because we want to do our own thing.

But we cannot faithfully serve God if we are not submitted to His will and His way. We may act like a Christian and go to church every time the doors are opened, but outside those four walls we concentrate on doing our own thing and we never consult God unless there is a crisis.

When God leads, He does not intentionally send you out on a limb to twist in the wind. He has a plan, and it is for good and not for evil. He knows your nature, your flaws and your hang-ups. God knows what you can handle and what you cannot.

This week practice letting God lead. Ask Him to take the leadership role once again in your mind, your will, and your emotions. Ask His opinion about every decision you have to make, big or small, and you will be surprised at His wisdom.

> *They shall come with weeping, and with supplications will I lead them: I will cause them to walk by the rivers of waters in a straight way, wherein they shall not stumble.*
> *Jeremiah 31:9*

A PHONY HAS NO TESTIMONY

IF DA HEAD OF DE FISH STINKS,
THE WHOLE FISH STINKS.
— DOMINIC LICCIARDELLO

This statement of my dad's is a word of wisdom. It is a simple phrase, but has a lot of truth for us today — deliver us from evil! If Jesus is not Lord of your whole being, then you are in trouble and will not have a powerful testimony. If you are not practicing what you preach in every area of your life, you will not be an effective witness. When your lifestyle does not reflect the teachings of Christ, you will be seen as a phony.

> *Let the word of Christ dwell in you richly in all wisdom.... And whatsoever ye do in word or deed, do all in the name of the Lord Jesus, giving thanks to God and the Father by him.*
>
> *Colossians 3:16-17*

No matter what language you speak, your actions will always speak louder than your words. You can preach Jesus to the world, but if His Word has not changed your thinking and your behavior, then you might as well save your breath. God doesn't want lip service; He wants heart service. If your head is full of things of the world, then your plans and schemes will reflect your faulty thinking. Do not expect to reach the lost for Christ if you have "stinking thinking."

You may think that others do not see the real you, but more often than not, you expose your true nature by your actions and words. The Word tells us in Luke 6:45 that what we are full of we will manifest. Sooner or later you will give yourself away. You may know the "plan" of salvation, but do you reflect the character of the "Man" of salvation?

Examine your heart this week. Are you a phony, or are you a godly, living, breathing example of all that you say?

> **A TRUE LEADER IS A MODEL FOR HIS FOLLOWERS.**
> — MYLES MUNROE

MISSIONE D'ITALIANO

Hey, I'm Italian — what more can I say?

THE ROMAN ROAD, OR THE ITALIAN WAY TO JESUS

If you want to lead someone to Jesus, take them down the "Roman Road!" It was written by my home boy, an Italian guy named Paul. (Yes, he was a Jew, but he was also a Roman citizen.) Everything you need for your mission can be found in the book of the Italians — I mean Romans. So here's the Italian version of leading a person to the Lord:

I. **INTRODUCTION**

    A. Yo, my name is Carman. (Carman works for me, you might want to use your own name!) What's your name? (Unless you already know them, of course!)

    B. Ask questions.

       1. Do you ever give much thought to spiritual things?

       2. Have you come to the place in your life where you know for sure you would go to heaven when you die? (If they say no, be prepared to show them how they can be sure they would go to heaven.)

II. The Roman Road — "The Bible says..."

    A. Heaven is a free gift — Romans 6:23

    B. All have sinned — Romans 3:23

    C. The wages of sin is death — Romans 6:23

    D. But Christ paid our penalty — Romans 5:8

    E. God asks us to believe — John 3:16

    F. Confess and believe — Romans 10:9-10

    G. You shall be saved — Romans 10:13

III. The Commitment

    A. Does this make sense to you?

    B. Would you like to receive God's gift of eternal life and know for sure that you will go to heaven when you die?

    C. Pray with me.

    1. Forgive me for my sin.

    2. I believe Jesus Christ died for me and was raised from the dead by God the Father.

    3. I now receive Jesus as my Lord and Savior.

TAKE OFF YOUR HAT

HERE RESTS IN HONORED GLORY
AN AMERICAN SOLDIER KNOWN
ONLY TO GOD.
— TOMB OF THE UNKNOWN SOLDIER

I recently discovered that the Romans (my people) taught the world the importance of demonstrating servanthood. The early Italians viewed the head covering as an emblem of social or political superiority. When an Italian man tipped his hat to a passerby, it was a sign of servitude.

Since the 1950s our dress code in America has become more relaxed, but before that men almost always wore hats. When they removed them or tipped them, it was a sign of respect or servanthood. In the past we had familiar phrases such as "with hat in hand," and "I take my hat off to him." These expressions reflected the understanding of this concept of servanthood.

Jesus taught His disciples the importance of servanthood as a means to reach the lost. Unfortunately, too many of us today want to be served; we do not want to be servants. We want to be up front, noticed, and acclaimed. Just as the tradition of showing respect by removing or tipping one's hat has almost disappeared, so has the tradition of servanthood by those who call themselves Christians.

I call an attitude of servanthood "the silent witness." If you are helpful on your job, an attentive listener to friends, or the one who reaches out to help someone who has dropped their school books in the hallway, you have become a servant. If you can see a need and meet it before you are asked, then you have mastered servanthood.

If this is an area you are lacking, practice "taking off your hat" this week. Each day commit yourself to one random act of kindness. Take out the garbage without being asked — do something that is not already required of you. Remember, to reach the world you must first be like Jesus, the greatest servant of all.

Well done, thou good and faithful servant: thou hast been faithful over a few things, I will make thee ruler over many things.
Matthew 25:21

SLAM

S ometimes the devil just needs to be told off and slammed with the Word. This one is for believers who want to exercise some spiritual muscle.

YOU SAID THAT I WOULD STUMBLE
YOU SAID I WOULDN'T LAST
BUT YOU WAS WRONG
YOU SAID THAT I WOULD CRUMBLE FROM ALL THAT'S
        IN MY PAST
BUT YOU WAS WRONG

YOU TRIED TO BREAK ME, TRIED TO SHAKE ME
TRIED TO TAKE ME WITH YOUR LIES
YOU TRIED TO DROP ME, TRIED TO STOP ME
TRIED TO CHOP ME DOWN TO SIZE

YOU TRIED TO CRUSH ME, TRIED TO HUSH ME
TRIED TO RUSH ME AND ATTACK
BUT JESUS CHRIST IS IN MY LIFE
AND NOW I COMIN' BACK 'CAUSE I CAN...

SLAM TEMPTATION WITH THE WORD
I CAN SLAM EACH LIE THAT I HAVE HEARD
I CAN SLAM THE DEVIL ON HIS BACK
THE ROD OF GOD WILL STOP THE ATTACK
IN MY MIND THERE IS NO FEAR
IN MY MIND THERE IS NO DOUBT

YES, I AM THAT CHRISTIAN THAT HELL WARNED
    YOU ABOUT
NOT ONLY CAN I DANCE, NOT ONLY CAN I SHOUT
BUT I CAN SLAM

YOU TOLD ME IT WAS USELESS
THAT I WOULD NEVER CHANGE
BUT YOU WAS WRONG
YOU TOLD ME IT WAS HOPELESS
THAT I NEVER WOULD GET SAVED
BUT YOU WAS WRONG

YOU TRIED TO DRUG ME UP, TRIED TO SLUG ME
TRIED TO PLUG ME UP WITH GUILT
YOU TRIED TO SHOOT ME, TRIED TO LOOT ME
TRIED TO BOOT MY MIND ON TILT
YOU TRIED TO KILL ME, TRIED TO STILL ME
TRIED TO BILL ME FOR MY SIN

BUT THE BLOOD HAS WASHED ME CLEAN

SINCE I'VE BEEN BORN AGAIN

I SHO CAN…

STOPPING EVIL

> FREEDOM IS THE NATURAL CONDITION
> OF THE HUMAN RACE, IN WHICH THE
> ALMIGHTY INTENDED MEN TO LIVE.
> THOSE WHO FIGHT THE PURPOSE OF
> THE ALMIGHTY WILL NOT SUCCEED.
> THEY ALWAYS HAVE BEEN,
> THEY ALWAYS WILL BE, BEATEN.
> — ABRAHAM LINCOLN

When you step out in faith to tell people about Jesus and get them free, the devil will come against you with every evil tactic, planting fearful and intimidating thoughts in your mind and stirring up your emotions. This is not a great feeling, but I can tell you that what Lincoln said is true: Anyone who opposes God will be defeated. They cannot win.

One way to slam the devil when he comes against you like that is to make certain your head is covered with the helmet of salvation (see Ephesians 6:17) and you have applied the blood of Jesus to your circumstances (see Revelation 12:11). Remind yourself how you got saved, all the great things God has done for you, and how you are His child and He loves you. You will break any hold the enemy would try to have on you, and freedom and peace will flood your soul.

> ***Submit yourselves therefore to God. Resist the devil, and he will flee from you.***
>
> *James 4:7*

"Submit yourselves to God" means to immediately reject any thoughts of doubt or torment and turn to your heavenly Father for wisdom. Get *His* strategy to fight the evil that has attacked you. Then you can turn around and "resist" — or slam — the devil with God's Word and His power behind you. He will run away from you like a cockroach when you turn the lights on in a dark room!

But that's not the end of it. Now that you are free from whatever sin or bondage the devil tried to entangle you in, you can turn the tables and begin to torment *him!* Go out and tell someone your testimony, get *them* saved and set free. Believe me, it's a whole lot easier — and more fun — to carry out the mission when you're free!

YOU CAN'T LOSE WITH THE STUFF WE USE

> TYRANNY, LIKE HELL, IS NOT EASILY
> CONQUERED; YET WE HAVE
> THIS CONSOLATION WITH US,
> THAT THE HARDER THE CONFLICT,
> THE MORE GLORIOUS THE TRIUMPH.
> — THOMAS PAINE

When you look at American society today and everything that's going on around the world, with so many struggling to survive and experiencing the pain from evil, it appears that Satan is winning. But I believe we Christians have allowed the floodgates of sin and evil to come pouring in because we have failed to use all God's power to keep this tyrant OUT. When you see what the Bible says about him, you'll know what I mean:

They that see thee shall narrowly look upon thee, and consider thee, saying, Is this the man that made the earth to tremble, that did shake kingdoms; That made the world as a wilderness, and destroyed the cities thereof; that opened not the house of his prisoners?

Isaiah 14:16-17

Thou hast defiled thy sanctuaries by the multitude of thine iniquities...; therefore will I bring forth a fire from the midst of thee, it shall devour thee, and I will bring thee to ashes upon the earth in the sight of all them that behold thee.

Ezekiel 28:18

And he [Jesus] said unto them, I beheld Satan as lightning fall from heaven. Behold, I give unto you power to tread on serpents and scorpions, and over all the power of the enemy: and nothing shall by any means hurt you.

Luke 10:18-19

Satan is no match for Jesus and Jesus is in YOU! The devil is just an ash disguised as a sparkling angel; but you have the Holy Spirit inside of you. Decide right now to stand your ground and drive him OUT. You just can't loose with the stuff we use!

ANTIDOTE FOR SNAKEBITE

NEVER GIVE IN, NEVER GIVE IN, NEVER, NEVER, NEVER, NEVER — IN NOTHING, GREAT OR SMALL, LARGE OR PETTY — NEVER GIVE IN EXCEPT TO CONVICTIONS OF HONOR AND GOOD SENSE.

— WINSTON CHURCHILL

It is estimated that between 30,000 and 40,000 people die from snakebite each year, 75 percent in densely populated India. Burma has the highest mortality rate, with 15.4 deaths per 100,000 population every year. In South America about 4,500 people die annually from snakebite.

When Satan first troubled the peaceful existence of Adam and Eve in the Garden, he was judged by God. His punishment was twofold, one was immediate and one was to come later. First, God commanded Satan to crawl on his belly or to, "Bite the dust." Then He prophesied the coming of His Son, Jesus, who would crush Satan's head, or strip him of all authority and power.

Satan is slithering around the world today taking lives, stealing property, and destroying everything in his path — if we let him. But through Jesus Christ we have been given a divine serum called *authority*. The Word of God and the Holy Spirit are our heavenly antidote. With the Word and the Spirit, we will fight that old serpent and never, never, never give up until we win!

When you hear the old rattlesnake slithering up to your door, grab your serum! One look at you — filled with God's power and wisdom — and he will flee. If he's stupid enough to hang around, pull out your sword — God's Word — and cut him to pieces. Remember, his days are numbered!

And the devil, who deceived them, was thrown into the lake of burning sulfur, where the beast and the false prophet had been thrown. They will be tormented day and night for ever and ever.

Revelation 20:10 NIV

ALL IN LIFE

This pretty much sums up why I sing for Jesus. To me, using my talent to build the kingdom of God is the only thing worth waking up for.

A FORTUNE MADE, A GOAL ACHIEVED
BUT IN GOD'S SIGHT, WHAT DOES IT MEAN?
IF I DON'T GLORIFY YOUR NAME
THE THINGS I DO, I'LL DO IN VAIN
OH LORD, TO PLEASE YOU
IS WHAT I YEARN
HELP ME REMEMBER THIS TRUTH I'VE LEARNED

THAT KINGDOMS COME AND KINGDOMS GO
BUT THROUGH THE WORD OF GOD I KNOW
WHEN ALL IN LIFE IS DONE AND PAST
ONLY WHAT'S DONE FOR CHRIST WILL LAST

TO SACRIFICE AND REACH A STAR
BUT THEN LOSE SIGHT OF WHO YOU ARE
IS NEVER WORTH THE PRICE, I KNOW
TO GAIN THE WORLD AND LOSE THE SOUL
I KNOW NOW THAT YOU'VE TRIED TO SAY, LORD, TO ME
MY SPIRIT CAN UNDERSTAND
NOW, I CAN SEE

ALL OF ME

ALL — THE TOTAL ENTITY OR EXTENT OF. THE WHOLE. THE UTMOST POSSIBLE. EVERY MANNER OF. ANY WHATSOEVER. NOTHING BUT — ALL.

— DANIEL WEBSTER

Years ago there was a movie that featured Steve Martin and Lily Tomlin entitled, *All of Me*. It had a mystical theme that opposed the things of God, but I looked beyond the world's foolishness and saw a deep spiritual truth.

It was a story about male and female spirits living in the same body. There was constant conflict, because each one wanted control. The body could not even walk right — pay attention to this — because Lily Tomlin wanted to walk like a woman, and Steve Martin wanted to walk like a man. One of them would say something, and then a second later the other would say the opposite. When I saw that hilarious portrayal, these verses came alive in a whole new way:

> *A double minded man is unstable in all his ways.*
>
> *James 1:8*

With the tongue we praise our Lord and Father, and with it we curse men, who have been made in God's likeness. Out of the same mouth comes praise and cursing. My brothers, this should not be.

James 3:9,10 NIV

There is only one word that will do in serving God — ALL. If you have not given your all to Jesus, you are behaving just like that movie character — unstable in all your ways! Kind of cancels out your mission, if you know what I mean.

God gave His all when He gave His only Son. His Son gave His all for us on the cross. How can we give any less than 100 percent back to Him? And when we belong to Him completely, our lives become balanced and we can fulfill the mission He's given us.

What part of you have you been holding back — a relationship, an attitude of bitterness, rebellion, or a critical spirit? Have you surrendered your finances, your Sundays, and your daily walk? Make a list and ask Him to show you the way of surrender in these areas. He will help you to succeed!

WHAT WILL LAST?

I SAW ETERNITY THE OTHER NIGHT
LIKE A GREAT RING OF PURE
AND ENDLESS LIGHT.
— HENRY VAUGHN

Today society is possessed with improving the body and the mind. Universities are filled with those who hunger for knowledge. Students spend hours — and thousands of dollars — reading and listening to lectures to gain information that will improve their quality of life. And the physical fitness craze has become a billion-dollar industry with spas, gyms, and workout centers in every city. We spend hundreds of dollars on workout clothing and athletic shoes.

Yet many believers spend only Sunday morning dedicated to their spiritual growth. Our bodies get several hours of attention each day, but our mind is renewed and our spirit man built up only a few hours every week. Could this be a problem?

For physical training is of some value, but godliness has value for all things, holding promise for both the present life and the life to come.

1 Timothy 4:8 NIV

When life is over and we stand before Jesus, I think I can safely say that we will not be interested in what shape our physical bodies are in. And throughout eternity, I don't think we will be standing around discussing how we kept in good physical shape while we lived in our death-doomed earth suits. No, I think we will be consumed with understanding the truth of God's Word and drawing as close to Him as we can.

> **What good is it for a man to gain the whole world, yet forfeit his soul?**
>
> **Mark 8:36** NIV

How about a spiritual checkup? What are you doing to bring spiritual growth? You cannot achieve God's plan for your life without spiritual maturity. You've got to develop your faith muscle and your righteousness tendon — and that humility hamstring that tends to be weak when everything else is working good! It's ultimately your spiritual maturity that will carry you through in your mission.

SURRENDER

> AND UNTO HIM WHO MOUNTS THE WHIRLWIND AND DIRECTS THE STORM, I WILL CHEERFULLY LEAVE THE ORDERING OF MY LOT, AND WHETHER ADVERSE OR PROSPEROUS DAYS SHOULD BE MY FUTURE PORTION, I WILL TRUST IN HIS RIGHT HAND TO LEAD ME SAFELY THROUGH, AND AFTER A SHORT ROTATION OF EVENTS, FIX ME IN A STATE IMMUTABLE AND HAPPY.
>
> — ABIGAIL ADAMS

A friend of mine told me a tremendous story about her mother. She had been a nurse and missionary in Africa, helped translate the New Testament into the dialect of the tribe where she ministered, and spoke three languages. When she came home from the mission field, single and in her late thirties, she asked God for a husband and two little girls. God gave her both, and she was as faithful to fulfill those duties as she had been with her assignment in Africa. This woman was a trail blazer!

After her pastor/husband died, she continued to

raise her two young girls, imparting to them the truth she had learned from years of dependence on the Word of God. She often slept with her Bible on her chest, having fallen asleep immersed in God's Word. Later in life, as her mother lay dying, my friend laid her head on her mother's chest, longing for the godly wisdom she had once given so freely. To her surprise, her mother opened her eyes and began to sing, "All to Jesus I surrender, all to Him I freely give, I will ever love and trust Him, in His presence daily live. I surrender all. I surrender all. All to Thee, my blessed Savior, I surrender all."

At that moment, my friend saw so clearly the secret of her mother's strength, success, and joy: no matter what the circumstance, she was totally surrendered to Jesus.

> *I am crucified with Christ: nevertheless I live; yet not I, but Christ liveth in me: and the life which I now live in the flesh I live by the faith of the Son of God, who loved me, and gave himself for me.*
>
> *Galatians 2:20*

A CALL
TO ACTION

THE WILL

THE CHOICE BEFORE US IS PLAIN: CHRIST OR CHAOS, CONVICTION OR COMPROMISE, DISCIPLINE OR DISINTEGRATION.

— PETER MARSHALL

Every day you face a million choices, usually beginning with whether or not you will get out of bed! You have a choice whether or not to brush your teeth, eat breakfast, and go to school or work. You are always going to face decisions, because God created you that way.

You see, God already had angels in heaven to praise His name and obey His commands without question. But He wanted children, sons and daughters, who would desire to love Him and be with Him, who would want to talk with Him and walk with Him, and who would enjoy His beautiful creation with Him.

The real issue here is your purpose. God wants fellowship with you. He wants to be recognized as God and chosen as your friend. Today many recognize the existence of God, but they have not chosen to make Him Lord of their lives or pursued Him as their best friend. Their choice has been to continue doing their own thing, getting God involved only when they are in trouble and cannot fix it themselves.

In your mission, you can talk all you want about God, you can spout religious principles till you are blue in the face, but you will not influence anyone if you have not set your will to choose Jesus Christ above all other distractions of life. The decisions you make add up to the witness you are for the kingdom of God.

> *...choose you this day whom ye will serve;... but as for me and my house, we will serve the Lord.*
>
> *Joshua 24:15*

If you are going to encourage unbelievers to choose Jesus, then you will have to be choosing Jesus in your daily life, and they will see it if you do. Your mission depends upon the direction of your will!

THE WORD

> IN ALL MY PERPLEXITIES AND
> DISTRESSES, THE BIBLE HAS NEVER
> FAILED TO GIVE ME LIGHT
> AND STRENGTH.
> — ROBERT E. LEE

Words have power. They teach and they taunt. They destroy and build up. And they are used too frequently to say nothing at all. The old saying, "My word is my bond," has gone by the wayside. As a general rule in society today, you cannot trust another man's word. But you can trust the One who is *the* Word.

In the beginning was the Word, and the Word was with God, and the Word was God. And the Word was made flesh, and dwelt among us, (and we beheld his glory, the glory as of the only begotten of the Father,) full of grace and truth.

John 1:1,14

Jesus is the Living Word. The Word of God is alive! Sometimes I will read a scripture that I have read many times before, but this time it seems to leap off the page of my Bible into my spirit. Other times I will be sitting in a church service, listening to the Word, and something the minister says will begin to resonate in my spirit until I feel like I am totally transformed. Many of the songs I write have come from just such an experience. That happens because the Word is *alive*. It has just what you need, when you need it.

> **For the word of God is living and active. Sharper than any double-edged sword, it penetrates even to dividing soul and spirit, joints and marrow; it judges the thoughts and attitudes of the heart.**
>
> **Hebrews 4:12** NIV

If you don't have a Bible reading plan, get one today. You need the Living Word renewing your mind and feeding your spirit man every day. It's the only fuel that will give you the energy and road map for your mission! The Word has everything you need for life.

THE WITNESS

> **BUT YOU WILL RECEIVE POWER WHEN THE HOLY SPIRIT COMES ON YOU; AND YOU WILL BE MY WITNESSES IN JERUSALEM, AND IN ALL JUDEA AND SAMARIA, AND TO THE ENDS OF THE EARTH.**
>
> — ACTS 1:8 NIV

Jesus' last command to His Church before He ascended into heaven was to be His witnesses. Our mission was to be like Him on the earth, and He told us not to do a thing until the Holy Ghost came upon us. Obviously, the Holy Ghost has something we need to accomplish our mission — power. You cannot be like Jesus without power!

I believe there are two ways to witness: in word and in deed. If you witness in deed, you are "being" the Word. You are acting like Jesus. Then many times just *being* the Word will open the door to *speak* the Word. But however you have the opportunity to speak the Word, the power and anointing of the Holy Spirit has to be on it, or the Word becomes a dead letter — kind of like trying to paddle a canoe down a dry river bed!

The rain of the Holy Spirit waters the seed of the Word so it will grow in the heart.

Jesus told us to witness first in Jerusalem, which means where we live. People in our homes and neighborhoods know us best, so when they see our joy, that we have been drinking at the well of living water, they will want a drink of what we have been sippin'!

How is your witness? Are you full and overflowing with the love of Jesus? Are you living better today than yesterday? Can men observe your life and see God at work?

Hint: If you're not there, it's time to get into prayer. Jude 20 tells us to pray in the Holy Ghost, Paul tells us to pray without ceasing in 1 Thessalonians 5:17, and Jesus admonished us to pray always in Luke 21:36. Why? Prayer brings the power of the Holy Spirit into your life!

So now you know what you've got to do to get the power. Remember, hit your knees before you hit the streets!

THE WAY

> THE GOOD (IN THE UNITED STATES)
> WOULD NEVER HAVE COME INTO BEING
> WITHOUT THE BLESSING AND POWER
> OF JESUS CHRIST.... I KNOW HOW
> EMBARRASSING THIS MATTER IS TO
> POLITICIANS, BUREAUCRATS,
> BUSINESSMEN AND CYNICS; BUT,
> WHATEVER THESE HONORED MEN THINK,
> THE IRREFUTABLE TRUTH IS THAT
> THE SOUL OF AMERICA IS AT ITS BEST
> AND HIGHEST, CHRISTIAN.
> — CHARLES MALIK

A little girl in church had misunderstood the words of the song, which were, "I'm on my way to Canaan land." Her interpretation was, "I *want* my way to Canaan land." She sang it with great gusto, so people around her were laughing, but there was truth in her words. Most of us want things our way — and right away! After all, Burger King says we can have it our way. But what does the King of kings say?

When I hear someone say, "It's my way or the highway," I think to myself, "Man, have they got that right!" You see, if we choose our own way, it is really the low road of life. The "high" way, or the Most High way, is always the best way.

When we take our way, our vision is limited. We cannot know what lies ahead. The auto club may have outlined our journey, but they might not have the latest information. Your car may have an onboard guidance system, but it cannot protect you from dangerous road conditions. Only God can see the end from the beginning. He is the only One who knows where potholes, brush fires, and flash floods threaten.

> *Walk in his ways, and keep his decrees and commands, his laws and requirements, as written in the Law of Moses, so that you may prosper in all you do and wherever you go.*
> *1 Kings 2:3* NIV

This is our mission in America and around the world today: to walk in His ways. If we do that, we will achieve His greatest expectations and blessings for us, many will come to the Lord, and our rewards in eternity will be beyond our wildest dreams!

MISSION 3:16 SCRIPTURES

Joshua 3:16   That the waters which came down from above stood and rose up upon an heap very far from the city Adam, that is beside Zaretan: and those that came down toward the sea of the plain, even the salt sea, failed, and were cut off: and the people passed over right against Jericho.

1 Samuel 3:16   Then Eli called Samuel, and said, Samuel, my son. And he answered, Here am I.

Ezekiel 3:16   And it came to pass at the end of seven days, that the word of the Lord came unto me.

Proverbs 3:16   Length of days is in her right hand; and in her left hand riches and honour.

Ecclesiastes 3:16   And moreover I saw under the sun the place of judgment, that wickedness was there; and the place of righteousness, that iniquity was there.

Jeremiah 3:16   And it shall come to pass, when ye be multiplied and increased in the land, in those days, saith the Lord, they shall say no more, The ark of the covenant of the Lord: neither shall it come to mind: neither shall they remember it; neither shall they visit it; neither shall that be done any more.

Daniel 3:16 Shadrach, Meshach, and Abednego, answered and said to the king, O Nebuchadnezzar, we are not careful to answer thee in this matter.

Joel 3:16   The Lord also shall roar out of Zion, and utter his voice from Jerusalem; and the heavens and the earth shall shake: but the Lord will be the hope of his people, and the strength of the children of Israel.

Matthew 3:16 And Jesus, when he was baptized, went up straightway out of the water: and, lo, the heavens were opened unto him, and he saw the Spirit of God descending like a dove, and lighting upon him.

Luke 3:16 John answered, saying unto them all, I indeed baptize you with water; but one mightier than I cometh, the latchet of whose shoes I am not worthy to unloose: he shall baptize you with the Holy Ghost and with fire.

JOHN 3:16 FOR GOD SO LOVED THE WORLD, THAT HE GAVE HIS ONLY BEGOTTEN SON, THAT WHOSOEVER BELIEVETH IN HIM SHOULD NOT PERISH, BUT HAVE EVERLASTING LIFE.

Acts 3:16 And his name through faith in his name hath made this man strong, whom ye see and know: yea, the faith which is by him hath given him this perfect soundness in the presence of you all.

1 Corinthians 3:16 Know ye not that ye are the temple of God, and that the Spirit of God dwelleth in you?

2 Corinthians 3:16 Nevertheless when it shall turn to the Lord, the veil shall be taken away.

Galatians 3:16 Now to Abraham and his seed were the promises made. He saith not, And to seeds, as of many; but as of one, And to thy seed, which is Christ.

Ephesians 3:16 That he would grant you, according to the riches of his glory, to be strengthened with might by his Spirit in the inner man.

Philippians 3:16 Nevertheless, whereto we have already attained, let us walk by the same rule, let us mind the same thing.

Colossians 3:16 Let the word of Christ dwell in you richly in all wisdom; teaching and admonishing one another in psalms and hymns and spiritual songs, singing with grace in your hearts to the Lord.

2 Thessalonians 3:16 Now the Lord of peace himself give you peace always by all means. The Lord be with you all.

1 Timothy 3:16 And without controversy great is the mystery of godliness: God was manifest in the flesh, justified in the Spirit, seen of angels, preached unto the Gentiles, believed on in the world, received up into glory.

2 Timothy 3:16 All scripture is given by inspiration of God, and is profitable for doctrine, for reproof, for correction, for instruction in righteousness.

James 3:16 For where envying and strife is, there is confusion and every evil work.

1 John 3:16 Hereby perceive we the love of God, because he laid down his life for us: and we ought to lay down our lives for the brethren.

Revelation 3:16 So then because thou art lukewarm, and neither cold nor hot, I will spue thee out of my mouth.

About the Author

Carman Licciardello was born and raised in New Jersey and grew up in an Italian home of music and laughter. Carman played drums and guitar as a boy and began singing as a teenager. Drawn to the entertainment field, as an adult he began playing clubs and eventually performed in Las Vegas, where he gave his life to Jesus Christ. Shortly after he was "radically saved," he moved to Tulsa, Oklahoma. It was during this time that he matured spiritually and began writing songs for the Lord, traveling and ministering whenever and wherever he could.

By 1990, *Billboard Magazine* named Carman "Contemporary Christian Artist of the Year," and by 1993 his ministry was worldwide, with more than 50,000 people attending his "Music for Peace" crusade in Johannes-burg, South Africa. Because of the demands of his recording schedule, he moved the ministry to Nashville, Tennessee, in 1996. He has received many awards for his recordings, and many of his albums and videos have gone gold and platinum. However, his attitude and stance known throughout the body of Christ has always been to point people to Jesus and give God all the glory and honor.

Carman's bold and uncompromising stand for Jesus Christ in the entertainment industry, as well as his appeal to Christians of all denominations and unbelievers from all walks of life, remain the hallmarks of his life and ministry.

Books by Carman

Radically Saved
R.I.O.T. Devotional, Volumes 1 & 2
Raising the Standard
No More Monsters
Satan, Bite the Dust!

Additional copies of this book
and other book titles from
ALBURY PUBLISHING
are available at your local bookstore.

ALBURY PUBLISHING
P. O. Box 470406
Tulsa, Oklahoma 74147-0406

In Canada books are available from:
Word Alive
P. O. Box 670
Niverville, Manitoba
CANADA ROA 1EO